HUNTING THE
Whitetail Rut
GARY CLANCY

STOEGER PUBLISHING COMPANY · ACCOKEEK, MARYLAND

STOEGER PUBLISHING COMPANY
is a division of Benelli U.S.A.

Benelli U.S.A.
Vice President and General Manager:
   Stephen Otway
Vice President of Marketing and Communications:
   Stephen McKelvain

Stoeger Publishing Company
President: Jeffrey Reh
Publisher: Jay Langston
Managing Editor: Harris J. Andrews
Design & Production Director:
   Cynthia T. Richardson
Photography Director: Alex Bowers
Imaging Specialist: William Graves
National Sales Manager: Jennifer Thomas
Special Accounts Manager: Julie Brownlee
Publishing Assistants:
   Christine Lawton and Tina Talmadge
Administrative Assistant: Shannon McWilliams
Design & Layout: Peggy Archambault
Proofreader: Celia Beattie

Published by Stoeger Publishing Company
17603 Indian Head Highway, Suite 200
Accokeek, Maryland 20607

BK0408
ISBN: 0-88317-271-2
Library of Congress Control Number: 2003103842

Manufactured in the United States of America.

Distributed to the book trade and
to the sporting goods trade by:
Stoeger Industries
17603 Indian Head Highway, Suite 200
Accokeek, Maryland 20607
301-283-6300   Fax: 301-283-6986
www.stoegerpublishing.com

OTHER PUBLICATIONS:
Shooter's Bible
   The World's Standard Firearms
   Reference Book
Gun Trader's Guide
   Complete Fully Illustrated
   Guide to Modern Firearms with
   Current Market Values

Hunting & Shooting:
Advanced Black Powder Hunting
Archer's Bible
Complete Book of Whitetail Hunting
Cowboy Action Shooting
Elk Hunter's Bible
Great Shooters of the World
High Performance Muzzleloading
   Big Game Rifles
Hounds of the World
Hunt Club Management Guide
Hunting America's Wild Turkey
Hunting and Shooting
   with the Modern Bow
Hunting Whitetails East & West
Labrador Retrievers
The Pocket Survival Guide
Shotgunning for Deer
Taxidermy Guide
Tennessee Whitetails
Trailing the Hunter's Moon
The Turkey Hunter's Tool Kit:
   Shooting Savvy
The Ultimate in Rifle Accuracy
Whitetail Strategies

Collecting Books:
The Lore of Spices
Sporting Collectibles
The Working Folding Knife

Firearms:
Antique Guns
Complete Guide to Modern Rifles
Complete Guide to Service Handguns
Firearms Disassembly
   with Exploded Views
FN Browning Armorer to the World
Gunsmithing at Home
Heckler & Koch:
   Armorers of the Free World
How to Buy & Sell Used Guns
Modern Beretta Firearms
Spanish Handguns
The Ultimate in Rifle Accuracy
The Walther Handgun Story

Reloading:
Complete Reloading Guide
The Handloader's Manual of
   Cartridge Conversions 3rd Ed.
Modern Sporting Rifle Cartridges

Fishing:
Bassing Bible
Catfishing: Beyond the Basics
The Complete Book of Flyfishing
Deceiving Trout
Fishing Made Easy
Fishing Online: 1,000 Best Web Sites
The Fly Fisherman's Entomological
   Pattern Book
Flyfishing for Trout A-Z
The Flytier's Companion
The Flytier's Manual
Handbook of Fly Tying
Ultimate Bass Boats

Cooking Game:
The Complete Book of
   Dutch Oven Cooking
Dress 'Em Out
Fish & Shellfish Care & Cookery
Game Cookbook
Wild About Freshwater Fish
Wild About Game Birds
Wild About Seafood
Wild About Venison
Wild About Waterfowl
World's Best Catfish Cookbook

Wildlife Photography:
Conserving Wild America
Freedom Matters
Wild About Babies

Fiction:
Wounded Moon

To Nancy Clancy,
my bride of 32 years, who has for most of those years,
spent the last week of October and the month of November without me.
Nancy is not a deer hunter, but she darn sure knows
how important the rut is to the whitetail addict she married.
Thanks for keeping the home fires burning.

Contents

Introduction

As I write these words in the basement office of our home here in southeastern Minnesota, I am surrounded by the memories of past hunts. There are numerous photos of friends and family engaged in a variety of outdoor activities. Okay, hunting and fishing, but hey, that's variety. There is the first duck call my father ever gave me, a box of flies tied by my bride of 30 years, Nancy Clancy, a fistful of fly rods leaning in one corner, a homemade stick bow and crude arrows occupying another. On the wall are the mounts of 29 pretty decent whitetail bucks. I don't share that number with you to brag, or to complain. Many hunters have killed more or larger bucks. None have enjoyed the hunt more, although I hope that they all derived as much pleasure from their hunts and from the memories of those hunts as I did and continue to do. I share that number to make this point: Twenty-one of those 29 bucks were taken during the rut.

You might deduce from that, that I hunt more often during the rut than at other times of the season. This is not the case. Although I spend as much time hunting during the rut as I can and each season "chase the rut" across the country in an attempt to put myself in the right place at the right time, you cannot hunt whitetail deer from late August to the end of January, a full five months, as I do and hope to spend more than a third of your time hunting during the rut. So I actually spend much more time hunting during pre-rut and post-rut than I do hunting during the rut and yet, most of the mature whitetail bucks that have fallen to my bow or my gun have been accounted for during the rut. And that is my point and the sole reason for this book.

If you want to increase your odds of getting a crack at a mature whitetail buck, nothing else you can do will boost your odds as dramatically as will timing your hunt to coincide with the rut. That is assuming, of course that the area in which you have chosen to hunt has at least a smattering of mature bucks in the population. You can hunt the peak of the rut for a lifetime and never lay eyes on a mature buck, much less have an opportunity to kill one, if you are stuck with hunting in areas with very few, if any, mature bucks. Unfortunately, there are many such areas in the country today. Many deer hunters have no choice but to travel to get in on the best action that hunting during the rut can provide.

A whitetail buck can do some goofy things during the rut. Big, mature bucks, normally shy, secretive creatures, have been known to walk boldly across open fields in broad daylight when the rut is on. Some have picked fights with bulls, hogs and even tractors, when the testosterone rages through their system. Because of these isolated but well-publicized incidents, many hunters assume that all of the bucks in the woods have let their guard down during the rut. They think the hunting will be easy. Just find a comfortable stump, sit down and get ready, a good buck will come ambling along soon. It rarely works that way.

Deer hunters have been bombarded with information on hunting the rut. Magazine articles abound discussing rut phases, rub lines, hunting scrapes, making mock scrapes, the use of scents, deer calls and rattling, how to use a decoy, strategies for still-hunting the rut, hunting from ground blinds, tree stands, deer drives, moon phases, ad infinitum. In fact, it looks to me like there is so much information on hunting the rut available today, that many hunters are confused by this onslaught of solid information mixed in with more than the occasional conjecture or hype.

That is where this book comes in. A book devoted exclusively to hunting the whitetail rut. No myths, no guesswork, no well-intended but misguided information handed down from generation to generation of deer hunters as pure gospel. The rut is no big mystery. In the pages that follow, you will discover that simple truth. My promise to you is a book jammed with good, accurate, sensible tactics and techniques that you can put to use this fall to help you put the biggest buck of your life on the ground.

Gary Clancy
Byron, Minnesota

Chapter One

✦

TIMING
the RUT

ack when I was a kid, just cutting my teeth on Minnesota whitetails, the November rut was thought to kick off with the first good cold snap of the month. If hunting was slow, the old-timers all offered the same prognosis, "Just need some cold weather to jump-start them bucks," they would say. Today, that sounds pretty silly to a whole generation of deer hunters who have grown up knowing that it is the amount of daylight that triggers the annual rut, but back then, before the scientific community began studying white-tailed deer in a big way, the cold snap theory seemed to make perfect sense. After all, we hunters saw much more buck activity during a good cold snap than we did when the weather was warm.

Timing the rut is not an exact science. I cannot give you the exact date when all hell will break loose in your part of the world each year. But we can come close enough that you won't be wasting a week of precious vacation.

Even with all of the research being done on whitetail deer, timing the rut is still something of a mystery. Nobody out there can tell you in advance on what date and at what hour the peak of breeding will occur. Being able to read sign, like rubs and scrapes, will go a long way toward determining the timing of the rut in your hunting area.

Today, we know that the rut goes on regardless of the weather. It is simply the fact that daytime deer movement is greatly diminished in warm weather and accelerated in cold weather.

The rut occurs at roughly the same time each year because the "trigger" for the rut is daylight or more precisely something called photoperiodism. In every 24-hour period there is a varying amount of daylight and darkness. In the whitetail's world, changes occur according to the length of daylight. One of these changes, the one we are most interested in here, is what we call the rut.

WHAT ABOUT THE MOON?

The moon, I believe, has an important influence on the lives of many critters. For example, back when I did a lot of trapping, I came to expect my best catches of muskrat, mink, raccoon and beaver on nights during or around the full moon. And, like many fishermen, I have certainly noticed that, all other factors being equal, the best days (or nights) to be fishing are the three days on either side of a full moon and on the date of the full moon itself. Even humans react to a full moon. My wife, who is in the medical field, always hated being on call when the moon was full. "It will be a zoo tonight," she would say. "All of the crazies will be out and about." Usually she was right. So

I'm a big believer in the powers of observation. Those hunters who spend as much time as they can in the places the whitetail calls home and who pay attention to what is going on around them when they are in the woods are nearly always on top of what is happening in the world of the rut.

Timing is only one part of the puzzle. Now you must pick the best location to be hunting during that time. It's old news I know, but maps and aerial photographs can really save a lot of boot leather when it comes to locating potential stand sites.

it is certainly not news that the moon seems to have an effect on the whitetail deer as well.

There has been some excellent data collected during the past decade on how the moon influences whitetail rutting behavior. I've personally followed the work of my friend Charles Alsheimer with great interest. Charlie lives with deer year round. He is a student of the whitetail and has probably photographed more

whitetail deer than any man alive. He and his partner in this project, Vermont wildlife biologist Wayne Laroche, have spent literally thousands of hours gathering data which they feel confident can help them pinpoint rutting activity in any given year. This whole business of moon influence is very interesting. Indeed, entire books (some good, some nothing but conjecture) have been written on the subject of how the moon affects whitetail behavior. I will not try to cover that much

How much influence does the moon have on the timing of the rut? That mystery is still being unraveled. But one thing is for sure, the moon is a factor on the intensity of the rut.

The rut. Those two words make it a little easier to get out of bed on a cold, dark November morning. Those two words put a little extra bounce in your step as you hike to your stand. Those two words are what keeps you in that stand after most have called it a day.

ground here. What we are interested in is how, if at all, does the moon influence the timing of the rut or the intensity of rutting behavior? In very practical terms, the question I would ask is this: "Should you even bother to consider moon phase when planning your week's vacation for next fall?" My answer to that question would be a definitive yes. Here is an example of how I would use the moon phase to help me determine when to take my week's vacation.

I am going to assume that you want to

take your vacation during the two-week-long peak rut. Let's further assume that in the area of the country you will be hunting, that the peak of the rut generally occurs between November 8th and November 22nd. If the rutting moon, which is the second full moon after the autumnal equinox (September 21st), falls anywhere within those dates, I would plan my vacation around the full moon itself. Specifically I would want to be in the woods three days prior to full moon, the day of the full moon and three days after. If the full moon appears prior to November 8th, I would schedule my week's vacation for the first week of that two-week period. If the full moon appears after November 22nd, I would take vacation the last week I suggest this strategy, because my experience with the moon during the rut has been similar to that of many other serious whitetail hunters with whom I stay in contact, or talk to each year while doing seminars at deer shows around the country. It seems that the November full moon tends to have a definite pull on not so much the timing of the rut, but rather the intensity. If the

Only during the rut.

Peak Rut Dates

STATE	DATES
ALABAMA	JANUARY 18-22
ARKANSAS	NOVEMBER 18-25
COLORADO	NOVEMBER 15-20
CONNECTICUT	NOVEMBER 19-25
DELAWARE	NOVEMBER 7-15
FLORIDA	NORTH: DECEMBER 30-JANUARY 6
	CENTRAL: JANUARY 6-13
	SOUTH: JANUARY 22-28
GEORGIA	NORTH & CENTRAL: NOVEMBER 10-15
	SOUTH: MID-NOVEMBER TO MID-DECEMBER
IDAHO	NOVEMBER 10-15
ILLINOIS	NOVEMBER 10-20
INDIANA	NOVEMBER 14-16
IOWA	NOVEMBER 13-18
KANSAS	NOVEMBER 10-15
KENTUCKY	NOVEMBER 15-17
LOUISIANA	SOUTHWEST: OCTOBER 15
	NORTHWEST: NOVEMBER 15
	EASTERN: JANUARY 1
MAINE	NOVEMBER 12-18
MARYLAND	NOVEMBER 10-16
MASSACHUSETTS	NOVEMBER 12-15
MICHIGAN	NOVEMBER 8-15
	U.P: OCTOBER 26-NOVEMBER 5
MINNESOTA	NOVEMBER 7-11
MISSISSIPPI	NORTH: DECEMBER 7-23
	SOUTH: JANUARY 11-18
MISSOURI	NOVEMBER 10-20
MONTANA	NOVEMBER 10-16
NEBRASKA	NOVEMBER 10-15
NEW HAMPSHIRE	NOVEMBER 10-20
NEW JERSEY	NOVEMBER 15-17
NEW MEXICO	MID-NOVEMBER
NEW YORK	NOVEMBER 6-17
NORTH CAROLINA	LOWER COASTAL: NOVEMBER 23
	UPPER COASTAL: NOVEMBER 7
	PIEDMONT: NOVEMBER 18
	MOUNTAIN: DECEMBER 5
NORTH DAKOTA	NOVEMBER 15-20
OHIO	NOVEMBER 14-16
OKLAHOMA	NOVEMBER 14-19
OREGON	NOVEMBER 13-18
PENNSYLVANIA	NOVEMBER 12-18
RHODE ISLAND	NOVEMBER 8-13
SOUTH CAROLINA	NOVEMBER 23-30
SOUTH DAKOTA	NOVEMBER 15-20
TENNESSEE	NOVEMBER 18-21
TEXAS	WEST: DECEMBER 1-7
	HILL COUNTRY: NOVEMBER 15-20
	SOUTH: DECEMBER 10-17
VERMONT	NOVEMBER 13-18
VIRGINIA	NOVEMBER 16-21
WASHINGTON	NOVEMBER 10-15
WEST VIRGINIA	NOVEMBER 13-18
WISCONSIN	NOVEMBER 3-8
WYOMING	NOVEMBER 15-20

full moon appears during that traditional two-week peak rut period, you are in for some serious, full-blown rutting action. Don't miss it. If the full moon appears on the front side of the rut, the first week will be the week of peak activity. And if the full moon appears on the back side of the rut, you can expect good action during that last week of the rut, but you can also count on the rut being more drawn out than normal.

When trying to predict the hottest week to be hunting, remember this: You can pick the right dates and still strike out if the weather throws you a curve ball. Warm weather shuts down daytime rutting activity no matter what the calendar might read. The best you and I can do is use all of the information available to us to pick the best possible dates and then go hunting.

To make that task a little easier for you, I have included peak rut dates for each state. You will notice that in some states, the dates vary according to various regions of the state. Use these dates as a starting point for determining which days will give you your best opportunity for making contact with a good buck.

I killed this buck on the morning of November 18th in northern Saskatchewan. I had hunted ten days and seen only a handful of bucks. And then on November 17th, somebody flipped the switch. That is how it often happens. Be there.

Chapter Two

The MYSTERIOUS MID-OCTOBER MINI-RUT

What if I told you that each October there is a burst of rutting activity in the middle of that month? Would you just laugh at me? Would you sadly shake your head and figure that poor old Clancy has spent a few too many hours in a tree stand? I would not blame you if you did. But the truth is that for the past 20 years, during most of those years, I have witnessed some serious, albeit short-lived rutting activity in mid-October, which, of course, is nearly a month before peak rut. This early rut provides a wonderful opportunity for some great whitetail action, but few bowhunters are taking advantage of it, simply because they do not know it is happening.

The reason why many hunters are not aware of what I call "the mid-October mini-rut" is that when most hunters witness some rutting

Because the mid-October flurry of rut activity is often localized, it is a good idea to spend time scouting and glassing to try to pinpoint hot spots before moving in.

action in mid-October, they simply write it off as a fluke event. Then, too, outdoor writers like myself, who have been aware of this October rut action, have been reluctant to write about it. After all, it is asking the reader to take quite a leap of faith.

At first, when I began to notice some rutting activity around the middle of October, I, like many others, considered it to be just some very localized abnormal behavior. I know that there are always some does that are bred outside of the two-week-long peak rut period, so it was not inconceivable to me that on occasion a doe could enter estrous a month early. But when I began to observe rutting behavior about the same time each October, I could no longer write it off as simply abnormal behavior. I wondered if other bowhunters had observed what I had been seeing. So I asked them.

If you know a serious bowhunter, or perhaps are in that class yourself, you know that these men and women tend to be a closed-mouthed-bunch. I'm talking about the best of the best, not the wannabes who spend more time bragging about how good they are than they do actually hunting. The very best whitetail hunters don't hunt to gain the approval or accolades of their peers. They just quietly go on about the business of taking a really good buck or

I like stands where I can see a long way during the period. A power line right-of-way like this allows me to see a long distance and determine if there is any mid-October rut activity happening.

two every season. I am fortunate to know a number of these archers and when I began questioning them about the breeding activity that I was observing in mid-October and started asking them whether they had been watching the same thing, most reluctantly confessed that they had been onto this early rut for a long time. A couple just gave me a sly, knowing smile and changed the subject.

Bowhunters can take advantage of the mid-October mini-rut by hunting areas that contain abundant whitetail food sources such as white oak acorns.

In the coulee country of western Wisconsin, hard against the waters of the Mississippi River, Tom Indrebo and his wife Laurie run an outfitting business specializing in whitetail deer called Bluff Country Outfitters. You may have heard of it. Tom has quite a reputation among serious bowhunters for putting his guests onto some very big bucks. Tom does not have a degree in wildlife biology, but he knows as much about whitetail deer as any man I've ever met. Tom and Laurie's farm is whitetail central in western Wisconsin. Hunters and whitetail nuts are constantly dropping by to show Tom deer they have killed, sheds they have found or just to swap stories. Tom and Laurie have been friends of mine for a long time, and sometimes when I do not feel like making the 80-mile drive home from the little farm I lease in Buffalo County, Tom and Laurie are kind enough to provide me with a hot meal and a warm bed for the night.

One cool evening, October 13, 1998, to be precise, I showed up at the door an hour after dark and was ushered in to sit at the big table where a half-dozen bowhunters and Tom were having supper. I filled a plate and listened to the stories from all of the other hunters and then later, when the others had retired to their cabins, I told Tom what had happened to me that evening.

I described to Tom how I had gotten to my stand on a little oak flat where the white oaks were loaded with acorns. I told him how at 3 p.m., the first deer, a doe and twin fawns, showed up. Pretty common.

But what happened next is not common for October 13th. A lone doe came hurrying down the ridge and behind her I could hear a buck grunting. The doe skidded to a stop 20 yards from the base of the oak in which I perched. I could see that she was an old gal. She had that long-neck and Roman-nosed look older does get. Her back was a little bowed too. The buck behind her turned out to be a scraggly little seven-pointer but he sure had big ideas. The old doe kept trying to eat, but the little buck just kept slinking up on her, head real low like they do when they've got something on their minds. The doe would scoot off and the buck would stop and sniff where she had been standing. Once the doe urinated and the buck hurried over, stuck his nose to the dirt and then lifted his head high and curled his lip to capture the scent. Before long, another buck showed up and then another. I get pretty fussy sometimes when hunting places with good potential for really big bucks and since none of the three were what I was looking for, I just sat back and enjoyed the show as the three young bucks took turns harassing the old doe. Just before dark another buck, a larger two-and-a-half-year-old, joined in the game. Then with the last light fading, I saw Mr. Big. I tried to grunt him in, but there was so much grunting going on from the other bucks that he never paid any attention to my grunts. None of the other bucks had done any scraping or rubbing the entire

time I watched them, but the big buck made three scrapes within just a few minutes and took another minute or two to work over a wrist-thick maple sapling. It was too dark to shoot by this time, so I just hung up my bow and watched him through my binoculars. After he finished with that little maple tree, he walked stiff-legged out toward the doe. The other bucks just kind of made room for him. The doe walked off with the buck's nose right on her tail.

"Now here is the real kicker Tom," I finished. "Last year, on October 12th, I was sitting on that same flat, in the same tree, when virtually the same thing happened. What's going on?"

Tom kicked back his chair, snared another cookie from the plate and spent the next hour sharing with me similar experiences both he and his guests have observed each October. Summing up our conversation, Tom closed with, "I'm convinced that on about the same date each October a few of the most mature does in the herd come into estrous. Because we are not talking about a lot of does, you are not going to see the widespread rut activity we expect in November. Rather, this activity is confined to the home area of the doe which comes into heat."

All of this makes perfect sense. Because there are only a few does in heat, those few does attract a lot of bucks. I've yet to see a hot doe during the mini-rut attract only one suitor. This situation is very similar to

Field edges are always good during this period because does are coming here to feed and if there is a doe in estrous, the bucks will likely encounter her here.

what happens during the so-called "second rut," which occurs about a month after the main rut. During this period, a few does that did not conceive or were not bred during the November rut will cycle back in for a second estrous. Also, in many parts of the country, a percentage of doe fawns will enter their first estrous about this same time. But because these numbers are nothing when compared with the November rut, each doe or fawn in heat at this time attracts a number of bucks.

Why I and others have most often noticed this October mini-rut action taking place in the same area year after year can probably be explained by food sources.

Fall foliage can enhance the effectiveness of camouflage when hunting the mid-October mini-rut.

The dominant doe lays claim to the best habitat and food sources in any given area. This is nature's way of ensuring the continuation of the species. Bucks, which in nature's scheme are dispensable, have to get by on less succulent forage. Even if an old doe dies, another doe, probably one of her mature daughters, will take over as the matriarchal doe and lay claim to the prime habitat. So anyplace where you have the best food, you can figure that there is an old doe ruling the roost. Since it appears that only old does enter into this early estrous, these prime food sources are the places to look for this early rut action.

OCTOBER 12-16 ARE THE MAGIC DATES

In the Midwest, myself and others have witnessed this brief flurry of breeding activity between October 12th and

October 16th. However, I will admit that there have been seasons when I have hunted these dates and not observed any rut activity. There are a couple of reasons why this does not surprise me. One, you have to be in the right place at the right time to get in on this mini-rut action. This is not a widespread occurrence as is the peak rut in November. On the years I have not noticed any rutting activity during these dates, I think the rutting action occurred on schedule, I just was not hunting in the right spot. Second, I strongly suspect that this brief October fling is tied into the moon just as the main rut is. I am convinced, as are many hunters, that the moon plays a role in rutting activity during the November rut. This being the case, it makes sense that the mini-rut in October is also influenced by October's full moon.

The October mini-rut is prime time for a young hunter to take that first good buck. The weather is nice and often the kids are on school break about the same time.

It is possible that the influence of the moon sometimes results in an earlier or slightly later October mini-rut and that on the years when I did not notice rutting activity during that October 12-16 period, the action simply occurred a few days earlier or later that year.

Where should you concentrate your efforts to take advantage of any early rut activity that might be taking place during this period? Food sources are my first choice for evening hunts. Doe family units will congregate on the very best food sources in the area at this time of the season. Each doe family group is made up of a dominant doe, a couple of her mature offspring and their youngsters. If you know of a place where such a family unit feeds or better yet a field being shared by several such family units, you will be in a good position if one of the old does enters estrous during this brief window of opportunity in mid-October. Remember, only a very small percentage of does will enter estrous in October, so the more does you have on the food source, the better your odds.

In the mornings, I concentrate on hunting trails leading from the food source to the bedding area. Trying to hunt the food source itself is too risky in the mornings. If you blow the deer off of the food source in the morning, you may disrupt them enough that they will not return that evening or will delay their arrival until after dark. Either way, you lose.

There are a lot of unanswered questions regarding the October mini-rut. Why it occurs is anyone's guess. My theory is that by having the oldest does bred prior to the main rut, nature ensures that the best mothers will be bred by the dominant buck. During the November rut, when numbers of does are in estrous at one time, it would be possible for an old doe to enter estrous and either not be bred or be serviced by a lesser buck. This makes sense to me, but that does not mean it is on the money. But not knowing is alright. One of the things I enjoy most about hunting whitetail deer is that there is always something more to learn about this incredible game animal.

My personal data, and most of what I have gleaned from others in regard to the October mini-rut, has been based on observations in the midwestern states of Iowa, Minnesota, Wisconsin, Illinois, Missouri, Kansas, Michigan, Nebraska and the Dakotas. I am assuming that the timing of the October mini-rut would be similar in the Northeast. Whether or not an October mini-rut even occurs in the southern states, I do not know. I suspect that because the rut in many regions of the South is spread out over a longer period than it is in the northern states, pinpointing an October mini-rut, if one occurs at, all would be very difficult.

The October mini-rut is not to be compared to the main rut in November. Rut activity during the October mini-rut is

This fence post had been rubbed nearly in two by October 15th when I took this picture.

very localized and involves only a few animals. During the November rut, the activity is spread out and all of the mature animals, bucks and does, get in on the action. However, with that said, there is no doubt in my mind that each October a few whitetail deer engage in some serious breeding behavior without the majority of bowhunters ever realizing that it is taking place. I would be remiss if I were to write a book on hunting the whitetail rut and not include this information.

Chapter Three

HUNTING *the* SCRAPING PHASE *of the* PRE-RUT

Most of the books and magazine articles on hunting the rut only break the rut down into two main periods, namely, the chase phase (also sometimes referred to as the seeking phase) and the breeding phase. The period of time when bucks are most aggressively making scrapes is usually lumped under the heading of pre-rut. Then when things really get cranked up and the bucks are checking scrapes several times a day, the definition changes to late pre-rut. That has always been confusing to me and it probably is to many of you too. Scraping behavior is definitely rut related and I toyed with the idea of just making the period when bucks are really scraping up a storm part of the rut itself, but then I thought that might be a bit egotistical on my part and even more confusing to many reading this book.

In most places, the scraping phase of the pre-rut is over by the time the gun season opens, but if it is not where you hunt, count yourself lucky and take full advantage of it.

Decoying, calling, rattling, they all work and work well during the scraping phase.

So, I have decided to just go ahead and leave scraping tied to the late pre-rut, even though I do not personally believe it belongs there.

There. With that off of my chest, let's get right into this whole business of scraping.

Most scrapes are either oval or round in shape and two to three feet in diameter. Although I would not go so far as to say that you could judge the size of the buck that made the scrape by the size of the scrape itself, it is true that bigger bucks tend to make the largest scrapes. And, although the size of the hoof is not always an indicator of the size of the deer, usually a big buck has big feet, so I am always interested in the size of the signa-

ture hoof print in the scrape. Scrapes that are consistently "worked" or reopened are larger than most scrapes. By the way, various research studies have found that between ten and 50 percent of scrapes are actually paid repeat visits and reopened. My own research would indicate that the ten percent figure is low and the 50 percent is high.

You will on occasion find a scrape without an overhanging limb, but they are rare and not worth hunting over. The overhanging branch is the real communication center at any scrape. Many times I have watched bucks visit a scrape and spend five to ten minutes chewing, licking, nuzzling and rubbing their faces and antlers on the overhanging branch, while paying little or no attention to the scrape itself.

I hesitate to place scrapes into categories, such as community scrapes, breeding scrapes, primary scrapes, etc., because I tend to agree with research that indicates that all scrapes start out being equal. Some scrapes just happened to be pawed out in places where they attract the attention of a lot of deer. Some of those deer are does that are nearly in estrous, others are curious fawns. Some, of course, are bucks. A buck that happens upon another buck's scrape will nearly always work the overhanging branch over the scrape and will sometimes paw and urinate in the scrape itself. If the buck that visits is a mature buck, he may use the same overhanging branch and then paw out his own scrape right next to the existing scrape. When this happens repeatedly you end up with what is commonly called a "cluster scrape" or "scrape cluster." Many of them I have seen resembled huge four- or five-leaf clovers. A four-leaf clover is considered a sign of good luck in Ireland and in some other parts of the world and I certainly consider the discovery of a cloverleaf-shaped scrape to be a sign of good luck. These clusters are good places to hunt because in most cases at least two mature bucks are involved.

I've seen bucks paw out scrapes from heavy slough grass and on ground that was mostly rock, but given the opportunity, a buck prefers soil that he can easily work up and clear of all debris. Usually the ground will be fairly level as well. Because scrapes are a buck's way of advertising, it makes sense that most scrapes are pawed out in areas of high deer activity and in relatively open cover. Scrapes tucked back in dense cover, I believe, are the work of a buck taking out

some frustration while confined to his bedding area.

When I first started deer hunting, scrapes were thought to be places where does in estrous came to meet bucks. It is understandable how hunters and researchers could have reached this conclusion, since does do, on occasion, visit a

The pre-rut scraping phase is your best chance to really pattern a big buck.

There should be some serious rubs showing up about the same time as those big scrapes. If they are not serious, you are probably not dealing with a big buck.

scrape, and one of the functions of a scrape may be to advertise a buck's presence and his breeding status to the does. But most visits to scrapes by does (and fawns) appear to be more by chance than design. In the whitetail world, scrapes are not primarily places where boy meets girl. Rather, scrapes are complex signposts that are attractive to all deer, but are more attractive to bucks than to does or fawns. The precise function of a scrape may never be known, but researchers now believe that scrapes primarily serve as an expression of dominance directed primarily at other bucks. A scrape is a buck's way of saying, "I'm big, I'm bad and those girls are mine buster." Not much different than what takes place in bars all over the country on Friday nights.

Serious scraping activity kicks off about three weeks before the first does come into estrous. But many of you will no doubt be surprised to learn that some scrapes are made during spring and summer. No, they are not as big or as numerous as the scrapes made in October and November, but they are well worth searching for, because these spring and summer scrapes are invariably the work of a big, mature buck. Find them and you have found that buck's core area.

The same is true of the first scrapes found each fall. Find a string or cluster of scrapes a week or two prior to the time when scrapes start to show up everywhere, and once again odds are excellent that you have discovered the handiwork of the dominant buck in the area. Mature bucks will usually begin scraping in early October although I have often found their scrapes in September. The rest of the bucks do not get in on the action until the last couple of weeks of October.

Take the time to map out all of the early scrapes you find. If the buck that made them survives to the next year, he will paw out new scrapes in many of the same places. This is invaluable information.

While giving seminars on deer hunting across the country, I am often questioned by hunters who never find early scrapes on the property they hunt and discover few scrapes even during the peak scraping period. I hate to be the one to break the bad news to them, but what this lack of scraping activity signals is that the area they are hunting is probably not occupied by a mature buck. Scraping is an innate trait with whitetail bucks, a trait that improves with the age of the buck. Older bucks make many more scrapes than do younger bucks. A mature buck might make hundreds of scrapes, while a young buck only a dozen or so.

Some think that if there are no mature bucks in the buck population in the area that they are hunting, that a young buck will step up and be the man. It does not work that way in the whitetail's world. Sure, the young bucks will do the breeding if there are no mature bucks around, but they are not programmed at a young age to take over the scraping duties a mature buck would otherwise perform in a well-balanced herd. Sorry guys, but an absence of early fall scrapes and only a smattering of scrapes appearing in late October and early November is a sure sign that the area is not home to mature bucks. Sadly, this is not an uncommon scenario over much of the whitetail's range. In many states, heavy pressure on the buck population, especially where gun seasons are held during the rut when bucks are most vulnerable, leads to a high buck harvest and an impressive percentage of successful hunters, but leaves little hope for any number of mature bucks in the population. This, I believe, is a big part of the reason why so many serious hunters are purchasing or leasing hunting land. If state agencies cannot or will not work to establish a balanced herd, individual hunters will manage their own property in an attempt to do so.

I guess I've spent more time than most men my age sitting in tree stands waiting for deer to show up in places where I think that they should show up. Many of those hours, weeks really if I totaled them all up, hell, probably months, have been spent perched in stands overlooking scrapes. Yes, I've seen some bucks come to visit those scrapes, even killed a few of them as they pawed in the dirt or worked their antlers in the overhanging branch. But when I get brutally honest with myself, I've got to face the facts that

Many hunters consider the scraping phase of pre-rut to be the easiest time to pattern an individual buck.

when you factor in the number of hours spent hunting over scrapes against the number of buck sightings, the ratio is pretty darn pathetic. So pathetic in fact that for a couple of seasons I pretty much gave up on hunting over scrapes. I read a lot of research on scrape making and after seeing figures like 70 to 90 percent, depending upon which research paper I was reading, all buck visits to scrapes occurred during hours of darkness; I used those numbers as an excuse not to hunt scrapes anymore. But I didn't last. I was hiking into my evening stand on the little farm where I hunt in western Wisconsin, when I cut the first scrape. I tried to ignore it, but I could not and after a little snooping around I found a string of five more scrapes marching across that little oak flat. The oak flat is shaped like an egg and probably not much bigger than a softball field, so five scrapes was a lot. All of the scrapes were big and all were fresh—very fresh. I hung a stand in a double-trunk basswood between two of the scrapes and settled in to see what would develop. By the time I climbed down three hours later, I had seen four bucks work that line of scrapes. One was a scraggly little seven-pointer, but the other three were all nice bucks, two eights and a ten and all of them in that 120- to 130-inch range, the ten maybe a tad better. I drew on the ten when he squatted in the nearest scrape and then with my finger resting on the

Many scrapes are never revisited and others only at night. But some scrapes will be visited by bucks during shooting hours. Picking the right scrapes is key.

release trigger decided to wait. There are some real monsters in that area and with all of the action that afternoon, I just knew that an even larger buck would be along. As it turned out I was wrong, but that's okay, it was quite a show anyway.

The next morning I was back in that same stand and stayed in it until dark. I saw three of the same four bucks, but not the ten-pointer. Usually, I don't hunt a stand three days in a row, but as far as I knew I had not spooked any deer from this stand and the scrapes were hot, so I pulled another all-day sit the third day

*A portable stand allows you to quickly set up and
hunt wherever you find the best sign.*

and this time I was rewarded with seeing four bucks. Two of them were repeats, but the other two were different bucks. One of them, the smallest of the four, made three visits that day. The only mature buck of the four made his visit a few minutes after the noon whistle had blown in the little town across the river. I like hunting places where noon whistles still announce that it is lunchtime. In fact, I was digging a sandwich out of my pack when I heard him coming. I forgot all about food, reached up and slipped the Mathews from the hook. I had not seen the buck yet and did not know if I would be needing the bow, but I've learned the hard way to get the bow in my hands at the first inclination that a deer might be headed my way.

My first glimpse of the deer sent my heart rate climbing. He was moving steadily in my direction, coming down off of the high ridge and even from a distance, I could tell by the size and shape of his body that this was a mature buck. My first glimpse of bone sent my heart rate up another notch. It was just a quick glimpse, but what antler I had seen looked to be very heavy. I slipped the release onto the string, adjusted my feet on the stand platform, did a quick once-over of the bow and arrow to make sure all was correct and got ready for the shot. It looked like it was going to happen in a hurry. Like many mature bucks, this one was not actually taking the time to physically visit each scrape, instead he was just cruising by downwind, letting his eyes and his nose inform him of any interesting developments since his last visit to the scrape line.

Just before the buck momentarily disappeared into a small stand of cedars, I got the impression that something was not quite right, but I could not determine just what it was. When the buck emerged, it hit me like a hard right fist to the gut. The buck's offside antler beam was broken off just above the brow tine. I had maybe three seconds to make up my mind to either take the buck or let him walk. Over the years, I have shot two half-rack bucks. In both cases, things happened in such a hurry that I did not realize the buck was only wearing half a

rack until I walked up to the dead deer. In both cases, I was sorry that I had taken the shot, so I let the big one-antlered buck cruise on by.

It is action like that which has got me back to hunting over scrapes, but even so, I'll be the first to admit that I do not spend near the time hunting over scrapes I once did. The reason for that is that I now realize that timing is everything when it comes to hunting over scrapes. The reason why I nearly gave up on scrape hunting, was that I was spending a lot of time hunting over scrapes at the wrong time, or hunting the wrong scrapes at the right time. Let me explain.

THE RIGHT TIME TO HUNT SCRAPES

For years, I was guilty of hunting scrapes too late in the season. I believe, after talking with hundreds of other hunters who, like me, became disillusioned with scrape hunting, that this is the number one reason why hunters give up on scrape hunting. Luckily, knowing when to be hunting over scrapes does not have to be a guessing game. As long as you hunt in a state where the rut is a relatively short-lived, intense affair, you can determine the best dates for scrape hunting by simply calling the big game specialist for the state you are hunting and asking him for the breeding dates for whitetail deer in that state. The dates he gives you, let's just say November 10th to the 20th are what is commonly known as "peak rut." Many hunters mistakenly believe that the peak of the rut is a great time to be sitting over a scrape line. The truth of the matter is that it is a very poor time to hunt scrapes. Bucks rarely visit scrapes while breeding is under way and the few bucks that do bother to visit scrapes are invariably youngsters that are frustrated with their inability to attract and hold a doe for themselves. The best time to be hunting scrapes is during the days and weeks leading up to the commencement of actual breeding. In a state where the breeding dates followed our example of November 10th to the 20th, I would concentrate my scrape hunting from about the middle of October up to November 10th and would expect my best action on the scrapes to take place from say October 27th until November 6th. Many of you might be surprised at that November 6th date, assuming that hunting over scrapes would just get better and better as the breeding period of the rut grew closer, but in the whitetail's world, there comes a time, usually three to six days prior to actual breeding activities when bucks go into what is commonly referred to as the "chase phase" of the rut. During this hectic period, bucks are so beside themselves that instead of routinely patrolling scrape lines, they are instead running all over giving chase to every doe they see. This is not a bad time to be hunting over scrapes, but there are places I would rather be when the chase is going on.

HOW TO SELECT THE BEST SCRAPES TO HUNT

If you have been frustrated in your scrape hunting attempts, it may be because you are selecting the wrong scrapes to hunt over. Many hunters simply choose the most obvious scrapes, but in my experience, rarely are the most obvious scrapes the best ones to be hunting over. In good whitetail country that has a balanced herd, bucks will scrape along the edges of every field and clear-cut in which the does are feeding. These scrapes are easy to find and easy to hunt over. The problem with these scrapes is that they are nearly all made at night and visited at night. Unless you are fortunate enough to hunt an area where hunting pressure has little or no effect on the deer, field edge scrapes are the very worst scrapes to hunt over. Scrapes found in open, park-like timber are not much better. A mature buck is a shy, secretive critter. Such a buck is not too keen on taking a stroll through the park during shooting light. So as you may have guessed, my number one criteria for a scrape worth hunting is that it be located in fairly dense cover. I'm not talking some terrible tangle that even a cottontail rabbit has trouble navigating, but rather the kind of habitat with enough ground cover that a mature deer might just venture out into it while shooting light remains. These are the scrapes you want to spend your time hunting over.

During 30 years of sitting over scrapes,

A mature buck like this might make hundreds of scrapes.

I have never yet found a lone scrape that was worth sitting over and trust me, I've sat over a lot of them. I've seen lone scrapes the size of a hot tub. On one lone scrape on which we hung a surveillance camera, a single 24-exposure roll of film revealed that 21 different bucks had visited the scrape in a single night. We hung a stand there the next morning and I sat om the stand for three days straight and saw a total of three bucks and none of them were anywhere near the scrape. What gives? What gives is that lone scrapes are almost exclusively nighttime hangouts for bucks and your odds of intercepting a buck at a lone scrape, no matter how big, how torn up or how inviting it might appear are somewhere between slim and none.

I'll take a string of scrapes in or near heavy cover every time. A good scrape line sees more daytime action than does a big, single scrape.

Now let's say that you are really lucky and hunting an area in which you have multiple scrape lines to choose from. How do you decide which one to hunt? Take the one that is located nearest a suspected bedding area. Whenever possible, I set my stand as close to the suspected bedding area as I can. The reason for this is that the last thing that buck is likely to do in the morning before turning in is to give those scrapes one more check. The first thing that buck will do when he rises from his bed to begin a night of carousing is to check out his scrapes. And for those of you, who like me, often sit on stand all day, it is not uncommon for a buck to sneak out of the bedding area and check the nearest scrapes to the bedding area when he gets up at midday to relieve himself and do a little browsing.

A FEW TRICKS

I've also enjoyed good luck luring these bucks out of their bedding areas by doing some grunting, doe-bleating and rattling while perched in a stand over their scrapes. Sometimes, too, you intercept a buck which is just cruising by that you otherwise would never have seen. Sometimes I incorporate a decoy when hunting a scrape line, other times I do not. The main consideration here is visibility. A decoy has to be visible to approaching deer from a distance for it to be effective. If a buck is right on top of a decoy before he sees it, as often as not the decoy will spook the buck.

I always use scents when hunting over scrapes. Many times, when I hike into my stand I will drag a scent rag behind me to lay down a trail of doe-in-estrous scent to my stand. Often I go out of my way to drag the rag right through some of the scrapes. Then, I juice up the scrape or scrapes nearest my stand. If I'm in a hurry, I might just take a bottle of scent and squirt some scent into the scrape as I pass, but more often I will take the time to work some scent into the scrape with a stick and if I plan to hunt the scrape line for a few days, I will often bury one of those plastic, scent-impregnated, Buc-Rut wafers an inch or two under the soil in a scrape. This is a dirty trick that encourages bucks to pay repeated visits to scrapes. On the overhanging branches, I like to hang a Buc-Rut wafer or a scent wick saturated with forehead gland scent. The overhanging branch is more important than the scrape itself. Many times I have watched bucks work an overhanging branch for minutes and pay little or no attention to the bare earth beneath their hooves.

So, don't give up on hunting over scrapes. Just accept the fact that some-thing like 75 percent of all visits to scrapes are going to be made at night. Sure, that's a bummer, but hey, if my math is correct, that still means that one-quarter of all visits are made during shooting hours, and those are not bad numbers. Hunt the best scrapes at the right time of the season. Use rattling, grunting, doe-bleating and deer scents. And then be patient. You are not going to see a buck checking his scrapes every time you sit a stand along a scrape line. But when it happens, all of those hours of waiting are soon forgotten.

The overhanging branch is the main communications center at any scrape.

Chapter Four

The CHASE PHASE of the RUT

It was the second week of November, the 10th to be precise. I was bowhunting in northeast Iowa, a state with a well-earned reputation for growing numbers of big bucks. The morning was one of those you dream about. Clear, cold and nearly calm. It was one of those mornings when I could just feel it. I'm sure you know what I mean. This was going to be a really good day.

Sitting in my tree stand in the dark, waiting impatiently for shooting light, I could hear deer running in the timber below the ridge on which I perched.

Whenever possible, hunt all day when the chase phase is in progress.

It was so still that the deer sounded like they were right under the wind-twisted oak to which I had strapped my stand, but they were probably actually far below along the tired, little creek. The light was still murky when I heard the unmistakable sound of a deer coming my way. It was a doe. She burst out from the edge of the woods, darted into a Conservation Reserve Program (CRP) field and came running full tilt right at my tree, which was situated right along the seam where the tall switch grass of the field melted into dark timber. Right behind her came a hog-fat Iowa mega-buck. In an instant, the doe blew past my tree. The buck was plodding along 20 yards behind. I drew and grunted at the buck with my mouth to get him to stop. If he heard me, he sure didn't acknowledge it. I let out a loud blaaat! The buck never hesitated, just kept right on motoring. I panicked, swung with him until my left arm hit a branch and then punched the release. My arrow buried into the frost-coated grass a good six feet behind his fat ass.

I was kicking myself big time for even taking the shot, when another doe came running full tilt over a gentle hill in the CRP field and interrupted my ass-kicking. A pair of young bucks were hot on her tail. The trio darted into a finger of brush jutting into the field about 200 yards south of my perch and disappeared. All went quiet. An hour later, I heard deer running behind me. Looking back over my shoulder, I saw another doe being chased by a buck. They ran by below my stand in the heavy timber and then came squirting out that same finger of brush the threesome had run into an hour earlier. Through binoculars, I studied the buck as he hot-footed after the doe across the CRP. Not huge, but a nice buck, long tines but lacking the mass of a mature animal. I contemplated moving my stand to that brushy draw. After all, it seemed to be the exit and entry route for deer moving between the CRP field and the timber. An hour later, having seen no more deer, I moved my stand. Since I planned to hunt all day, I figured I might as well be in the best spot. Yah right! Guess where the next deer I saw walked? You guessed it, right under the oak I had just vacated. Nice buck too. By dark, I had seen three more bucks, although I think two of them were the same smaller bucks I had seen chasing a doe earlier. One of them ran a doe in circles around that oak in which I had spent most of the morning.

That's the chase phase for you. Lots of action, but trying to pick the precise stand location to best take advantage of that activity will drive you nuts.

WHAT IS THE CHASE PHASE?

The chase phase is a short-lived period right between the scraping phase and the breeding period. In the northern half of the whitetail's range, these two periods are well defined, because the breeding period occurs at a predictable time each year and is short and intense in duration. This is nature's way of ensuring that the fawns will be dropped late enough in the spring to miss those deadly spring blizzards, but not so late that the youngsters are too small to make it through their first winter. In the southern states, where it is not critical that does give birth during a short and specific period, the breeding

During the chase phase, every buck in the woods healthy enough to breed is on the prowl searching for a hot doe.

tends to be dragged out over weeks and in some cases months, making it impossible to predict the timing of the main periods of the rut, much less the chase phase.

In those areas with a well-defined rut, the chase phase occurs at the tag end of the scraping period and just prior to the first wave of does entering estrous. The bucks have worked themselves into a frenzy by this time. They are primed and ready for action. To ensure that a doe has a buck already on the hook when she is ready to be bred, does begin to give off scent signals a day or two prior to actually entering estrous. These signals are picked up by the bucks and the chase is on. Of course, the doe is not ready to stand for the buck yet, so the doe has to stay on the move constantly. When you get multiple does in this condition in your hunting area, you are in for a real circus. When it comes to seeing numbers of deer, both bucks and does, no other time compares with the short but intense chase phase of the rut.

Because the chase phase is short-lived, timing is critical. Fortunately, predicting

Any high vantage point should let you eyeball plenty of chase phase action during this period of the rut. But don't sit back and watch too long. During the chase phase, it is important that you make your move quickly.

when the chase phase will occur is not difficult. The peak of the breeding period occurs on roughly the same dates annually. Granted, the moon phase, the weather, herd condition and hunting pressure can all have an influence on the exact timing and the intensity of daytime movement during the breeding period, but the dates will not vary by more than a few days in either direction from year to year. I've furnished you with the dates of the peak of the breeding period for all states. Once you know that the peak of the breeding period is, let's say, November 10-20 in the state where you are hunting, you can bet that the chase phase is going to occur sometime in the week prior to the beginning of the peak of breeding or perhaps the first couple of days of the dates listed. In this case, I would be looking for chase phase action between November 6th and 12th. Don't expect the chase phase to last the entire seven days, however, a couple of days of non-stop chasing is the norm.

Like many other hunters, I like to see a

When the chase phase kicks in, you will know it. Overnight, tracks will show up everywhere.

lot of deer, so the chase phase is one of my favorite times to be in the woods. If you are in decent whitetail country, seeing deer is almost a sure thing. However, seeing deer is the easy part. Setting up so that one of those bucks saunters by within bow range is the frustrating part of hunting the chase phase. Whitetail deer are unpredictable most of the time, but when you've got a bunch of sex-crazed bucks spending the day chasing unwilling, frightened does, the unpredictability factor skyrockets. I don't have any sure cures, but here are some of the things that have worked for me.

Using a doe decoy during this period can be dynamite. Usually I prefer a buck decoy, but during the chase phase, because bucks tend to rush up to every doe they see, I've found that a doe decoy, or two, draws more attention than a buck decoy. Be sure the doe decoy is easily visible. Field edges, clear-cuts, logging roads, natural woodland openings and tree-studded pastures are all good bets. The more directions from which a buck can spot the decoy and the greater the

Bucks don't spend long bedded down when the chase phase of the rut is in progress, which is precisely what makes it such a great time to be hunting.

distance, the more bucks your decoy attracts.

Funnels and food sources are the two best places for a stand during the chase phase. Funnels are good simply because there is so much traffic during this period. Food sources are even better, because bucks know where the does are feeding and they haunt these places regularly hoping to catch a doe busily feeding. As you might suspect, the places where does are feeding is a super spot for a decoy.

I do a lot of calling and rattling all during the rut, but right now is the primo time to grunt in or rattle up a buck. The bucks are going bonkers and it does not take much to convince them that they are missing out on some hot action when they hear what they think is another buck giving the tending grunt or two bucks fighting.

Always hunt all day whenever you can during the chase phase. Sure, the action is most intense morning and evening, but bucks are cruising for does all day long during this period. If you are going to take a break, do it between about 1:30 and an hour before sunset; in my experience this is the period of least movement. I suppose the deer have to rest sometime, even during the chase phase.

Chapter Five

HUNTING *the* BREEDING PHASE *of the* RUT

The breeding phase of the rut is commonly referred to as the peak of the rut, or quite often simply peak rut. What that term means is that this is the period when the majority of does will be bred. The peak breeding phase of the rut lasts about two-weeks. Sure, there are some does bred prior to and after that two week period, but the majority of does will be bred during the hectic two weeks of peak rut.

If you can manage the time, plan to hunt both of these weeks. But if you have to choose one week or the other, you are probably wondering if one week has the edge over the other? In my experience, the answer to that question is yes. However, the qualifier is that it all depends upon what you are looking for. Let me explain.

Some bucks drive does into the thickest tangles they can find to protect the does from pesky interlopers like this little buck. Other bucks take the opposite tact and hold their does in wide-open country.

If you are looking for lots of action and hopefully a shot at a decent buck, then the first week is the one you want to be hunting. This is the week when all hell breaks loose in the whitetail's world. Does, often two or three at a time, are coming into estrous. Bucks, already beside themselves with systems overloaded with testosterone, frantically follow their noses to hot does and then compete with other bucks for breeding rights. Mature bucks cut a hot doe out of the herd and then spend every waking hour tending the doe and driving off younger bucks trying desperately to get in on the action. If it's action you crave, this is the time to be in the woods. In good whitetail country, it is not uncommon to see multiple bucks each day during that first action-packed week of actual breeding activity.

One November, while bowhunting in western Illinois during the first week of the breeding phase of the rut, my journal reminds me that in four full days of hunting I saw an amazing 41 different bucks. Yes, I hunted all day, every day, which I nearly always do during this period, but even so, that is a lot of bucks. My journal also indicates that I saw many of those bucks multiple times. In fact, I had to chuckle when I read this entry "...the same small buck I saw four times yesterday has picked up his pace. Today the year-and-a-half-old buck with the oddly shaped, easily recognizable seven-point

rack came around seven times. In fact, he has been by my stand so often, that he no longer even glances at my decoy. I'm starting to feel sorry for the poor guy!"

WHAT THE BUCKS ARE DOING

Bucks are doing exactly what they are programmed to do, namely procreating the species. In unbalanced herds, where does greatly outnumber bucks and where mature bucks make up a very small percentage of the buck population, all of the bucks will be getting in on the action. In more balanced herds, the mature bucks will be tending to the bulk of the actual breeding chores, while the young bucks frantically hang around, acting goofy and try, usually unsuccessfully, to get in on the action. In herds where there is competition between bucks for estrous does, there will be some nasty buck fights taking place during peak rut. You can also expect to find bucks ushering does off to some mighty peculiar places during peak rut. In farm country, it is not unusual to see a buck tending a doe out in the middle of a 500-acre field of soybean stubble. Along the river bottom country I hunt in southwestern Kansas, although there is plenty of buck action in the river bottom cover itself, some of the biggest bucks will spend most of the breeding phase of the rut sequestered with a hot doe they have pushed up into a cactus and yucca plant studded canyon, seemingly much more suitable habitat for mule deer. The only time these bruiser bucks will be found in the river bottoms is when they come down looking for another hot doe.

A buck will stay with a doe until she is no longer receptive, which is a maximum of 36 hours, but since it is unlikely that a buck would be lucky enough to find the doe just as she enters estrous, most white-tail liaisons are shorter-lived affairs. The equivalent of a one-night stand, I suppose. As soon as a buck senses that a doe is no longer receptive, he abandons her and goes on the prowl looking for another hot doe and it does not matter to him if it is midnight or high noon.

BEST TIME OF THE DAY TO HUNT

Simple. All day. Like I said, when a breeder buck is between does during the breeding phase of the rut, he has no choice but to search for another one. He is programmed that way. After all, a mature buck's purpose on earth is ful-

The peak can be a frustrating time to hunt. You know they are there, but because they are busy with does, just seeing one is sometimes really tough.

filled during this two-week period.

Forced to select the best time periods, I would rank the first two hours of shooting light as prime, ten to one as excellent and the last hour of the day as very good. If I were going to take a couple of hours off to have lunch and grab a nap (and I'm not), it would be from one to three p.m.

When I travel to other states to hunt, I often hunt on my own, but when I do hunt with an outfitter, I am always amazed at the number of hunters in camp who never hunt all day during this peak period. I am even more astounded when, instead of asking to be picked up at say one p.m., these same hunters invariably request to be picked up at eleven or twelve. That's a big mistake in my book.

BEST STAND LOCATIONS

I'm going to go politician on you on this one. Best stand locations for the breeding phase of the rut depends. What it depends upon is whether you are hunting with a bow or a gun. If I am hunting with a gun, even a short-range gun like a muzzleloader or slug gun, I will try to hunt from stands that allow me to see the most country. Bucks are on the move big time during this period and the more territory I can see from my stand, the better the odds that I will lay eyes on a few of those bucks. Even if they are too far away to shoot, just by seeing them, I might be able to adjust my stand location for later in the day or the next day, or I may, as I have done on numerous occasions, climb down from my stand and hunt the buck on foot. Cut-over areas, CRP fields bordered by timber, fence line crossing farm country, woodland marshes and sloughs, power and pipeline right-of-ways, senderos, depending upon where in the country you are hunting, any of these might offer wonderful opportunities for long-range observation.

The tending grunt and doe bleat are excellent calls to use during the breeding period of the rut.

A good map or better yet an aerial photograph of the property can help you determine the best places to spend your time during the breeding phase of the rut.

When bowhunting, if hunting over a decoy, which I frequently do during this period and which we will discuss in detail a bit later, I often opt for some of the same long-range vision stands just covered. Even though I am armed with a very short-range tool, if I can see a buck, even though that buck is far out of range, I have a chance of being able to get his attention with either a grunt call or rattling horns and directing his attention to my decoy.

Very often, however, I find myself hunting a stand situated in a funnel during this period. Let's say for instance, that you have a narrow band of timber connecting one block of timber with another. That's a deadly location during the breeding phase of the rut. Sure, a buck might cut across the open to get from woods to woods, but most will not.

In hill country, I try to hunt high in the mornings and low in the evenings. Both bucks and does tend to bed high and feed low. Ridge tops are favorite stand locations. Narrow ridges are not as good as ridges that broaden out into brushy flats. The more finger ridges that

Anytime the breeding phase of the rut overlaps with the firearms season, don't drop your guard when a lone doe comes by. Get ready.

intersect on one of these broad, brushy flat-tops, the better.

In midafternoon, I like to move to a food source. Bucks are going to show up wherever does concentrate during peak rut and in the evening, that means that they will be near a food source. It might be a food plot, a field of agricultural crops, usually soybeans, corn or alfalfa. Maybe there is a bumper acorn crop and oak flats are still attracting numbers of deer each evening. In the north country, it might be a clear-cut area growing lush with young, tender browse. Whatever the food source, find it, and then key on it for evening hunts.

One last stand location you never want to overlook during this hectic period is a water hole. Bucks work up a substantial thirst with all of their activity. They need to drink often to avoid dehydration. They will drink from creeks, rivers or even lake shores, but their favorite is a secluded little seep or water hole in heavy cover. My friend Tom Indrebo has gone through the effort and expense required to dig a number of secluded ponds on his property. Each season, Tom's hunters score on two or three big, mature bucks that come to drink at these ponds. The warmer the weather, the better a stand near water is going to be, but even in cool or cold weather, bucks still need to drink and drink often during peak rut.

WHAT CALLING TECHNIQUES TO USE

I like a tending grunt with a few doe bleats mixed in, You can use a good variable tone grunt call, like my favorite the H.S. True-Talker, to make both the tending grunt and the doe bleats by simply adjusting finger pressure on the reed, or you can use a straight grunt call for the tending grunts and a can-type call for making the doe bleats. Primos, Quaker Boy and H.S. all sell cans that you simply turn upside down and then back to right side up to produce a quality doe bleat.

Some hunters claim to have had excellent results with the snort-wheeze during this period of the rut, but I cannot vouch for the effectiveness of this vocalization from personal experience, since I have been reluctant to use it very often. The reason I have shied away from using the snort-wheeze is that the snort-wheeze is an intimidating vocalization. It is one buck's way of telling another buck that he had better make himself scarce PDQ or risk a serious ass-kicking! Sure, there are some belligerent bruisers in the whitetail world, just as there are in the human race, who will gladly respond to such an invitation, but I believe that such bucks are few and far between. From my limited experience with the snort-wheeze, it seems to intimidate more bucks than it attracts, so I'll stick to my tending grunts and doe bleats.

RATTLING POTENTIAL

There are many hunters who claim that the breeding phase of the rut is a poor time to rattle in bucks. The argument presented is always the same, that the bucks are not interested in responding to rattling now because they are preoccupied with breeding. I disagree. While I consider the scraping phase to be prime time for rattling, the breeding phase runs a close second. In fact, in those areas of the country where the buck-to-doe ratio is not out of whack and where herds are managed for numbers of mature bucks in the buck population, the breeding phase would take top billing when it comes to rattling. In South Texas for instance, where ranches are managed to produce herds with just such dynamics, rattling is superb during the mid- to late December peak rut. Everything hinges on competition between bucks for available does. If you have such competition, rattling will produce wonderful action during the breeding phase of the rut. On some of the better ranches, it is not uncommon to rattle in a dozen or more bucks per day and most of them will be pretty darn good bucks.

While hunting in western Canada during the last two weeks of November, which is peak rut along this far northern fringe of the whitetail's world, I depend heavily on rattling to bring bucks to me.

A lone doe during the breeding phase of the rut will almost always have a buck trailing her. He might be a half-hour behind, so stay alert.

Here, you are, in most instances, dealing with a very low deer density, often under five deer per square mile. Obviously, bucks here must do a lot of traveling if they hope to encounter an estrous doe. If a buck on the prowl for a hot doe hears the sound of antlers banging up in this country, he knows that there is a pretty darn good chance that the squabble involves a lady. Odds of that buck charging in to investigate are pretty darn good. A couple of the biggest bucks hanging on my wall could not resist the clatter of horns. The three biggest were killed on November 17th, 18th and the 25th. I'm sure glad I did not heed the advice of many who proclaim that rattling during peak rut is a waste of time.

Western Canada and South Texas are not the only places where rattling during peak rut will produce results. I've rattled up nice bucks during this period in states such as Kansas, Iowa, Illinois, Wisconsin, Montana, Mississippi and Nebraska that I can recall and probably a few that have slipped my mind. Longitude and latitude do not matter. What matters is herd dynamics. If there is competition between bucks for breeding privileges, rattling during peak rut will produce. But if, as is sadly the case in many parts of the country, all racked bucks, regardless of age, are hard pressed to service all of the does that come into estrous during peak rut, rattling now, or at any other time of the season, is an exercise in futility.

Whether you use a computer or a journal, keep notes on what you see during the rut and the dates when things are happening. This information will prove very valuable.

If you do decide to rattle during this period, don't be shy about it. Make as much noise with those horns as you can. I can guarantee you that, no matter how much brush you rake, no matter how hard you slam and grind those tines together, no matter how often or how hard you pound the antlers on the ground, it is humanly impossible to make as much racket as two mature bucks do when they get it on at this time of the year. Bucks don't mess around with each other when it comes to breeding rights. These are serious battles that often lead to serious injury and sometimes the death of one or both of the combatants.

DECOYING TACTICS

Both the first and second weeks of the breeding phase are excellent periods to be hunting over a decoy. Either a buck or doe decoy will work equally as well during this period, although personally I tend to rely more heavily on a buck decoy. I've not yet had a buck leave a doe to check out a doe decoy, but I have had bucks momentarily leave an estrous doe to try to put the run on my buck decoy. Besides, many of the bucks, which I decoy during this period of the rut, are first attracted to either rattling or calling, usually rattling. They are expecting to see another buck when they near the source of the sound they heard.

My favorite setup for the peak of rut is to use both a buck and a doe decoy. When logistics are such that I can drive to my stand with an ATV or my pickup, drop off the decoys and then go stash the vehicle a good distance off and out of sight, I will use two full-bodied decoys, but most of the time, I do not have that luxury or do not want to risk the noise and commotion driving to the stand creates. I often use one full-bodied decoy as a buck and a silhouette decoy such as a Montana Decoy or Martine Decoy as a doe. There is a bedded doe decoy on the market that I have used in conjunction with a standing buck decoy to give the impression of a buck standing guard over an estrous doe. You can also remove the legs from a Carry Lite full-bodied decoy or the Flambeau Redi-Doe to make it appear to be a doe that is lying down. Whatever it takes to project the image to any passing buck that there is a buck tending a doe. This setup will get the attention of any passing buck that does not have a doe of his own.

SCENT TACTICS FOR THE BREEDING PHASE OF THE RUT

Rarely do I ever hunt from a stand during the breeding phase of the rut without having layed down a scent trail to the stand site. I say rarely, because there are situations where I am able to approach the stand from straight downwind, when I do not lay down a scent trail. Although I am very fussy about controlling human odor, I do not tempt fate by encouraging deer to walk in my scent stream to the stand location. Most of the time, however, I will try to approach at an angle or crosswind, so that I can lay a scent trail down all of the way to my stand.

I've probably used at least 50 different brands or "flavors" of deer scent for laying down scent trails over the years. Yet, I can't share with you that is best, because I do not know if there is one which is better than all of the rest. Just because a buck or two follows a scent trail laid down with Old Stud Fooler, does not make that brand the best. How do you know that the same bucks would not have followed any one of a dozen or so different scents had they been used that day?

I'm also not sure if a doe-in-estrous urine-based scent is best, or if you are better off using a buck urine scent, or maybe a scent that contains glandular secretions. Again, I've used them all and have had some success with all of them. I've also had bucks step right over the scent trail I've laid down and never even acknowledge that it existed. So again, if I had the answer to what scent is best, I would share it with you, but I do not. My advice is to use your favorite scent if you have one and if you do not to do some experimenting. To give you a starting point if you plan to experiment with various scents, here are some scents with which I have had very good results when used for laying down scent trails: Primetime Interdigital Gland, Primetime Premium Doe Estrous, Martine's Interdigital Gland Lure, Martine's Pure Tarsal Gland, Buckstop 200 Proof and James Valley Wallhanger.

I generally hang four to six scent wicks (scent bombs) around my stand. I doubt that these draw bucks in from any distance, but I have had them grab the attention of a passing buck and that is important at this time of the year when bucks are difficult to stop for a shot.

Lots of big bucks have fallen during the peak period.

Chapter Six

The
WANING RUT

Like me, you probably start to get cranked up during the early pre-rut stages and really tuned up when all of that pre-rut activity heats up and boils over into some serious scraping activity. All of us know that our best chance of ever slapping a tag on a real bruiser of a buck is happening right now. We hunt as if we are possessed during the rut. We might go to work, but we are not really there. Our family finds us staring off into no man's land as we plot, dream and scheme of ways to outwit a big buck. And then, before we know it, the rut peaks. As quickly as it peaks, the intensity level falls off. Our enthusiasm does the same.

The waning days of the rut are not as much fun to hunt as are the scraping phase, the chase phase and the breeding phase, simply because you do not see nearly as many bucks. I've had a lot of days during this period when I never laid eyes on a buck. But what keeps

Big bucks cover a lot of ground in search of leftover does in estrous during the waning rut. Those bucks leave behind a lot of tracks.

me coming back for more is the fact that a very high percentage of the bucks I do see during the waning rut are mature animals. If you like to hunt for big bucks, you don't want to be ignoring the waning rut.

To understand why the waning rut can be so good for a real bruiser of a buck, it is important to understand what is going on in the weeks leading up to the waning rut.

It all starts out innocently enough. Sometime in late October over most of the whitetail's range, rubs begin to show up in good numbers and scrapes begin to magically appear overnight. The bucks are beginning to feel the effects of the increase of the hormone testosterone coursing through their veins. Rut preparations have begun. Now bucks that used to spend all day laying around chewing their cud tend to spend more of the daylight hours on their feet, doing things like making rubs, pawing out scrapes, checking out does and picking fights with other bucks. This means that our odds of laying eyes on one of these bucks has just taken a giant step forward. As October gives way to November, bucks spend more and more time each day on the prowl and finally, usually sometime

The firearms deer season coincides with the waning rut in many fine whitetail states.

during that first week of November, they can't stand it anymore and start chasing every doe they see regardless of whether or not the doe shows any sign of being in estrous. We call it the chase phase of the rut. Sometimes three or four of the sex-crazed critters get to chasing the same hapless doe around the woods. And then the first does enter estrous and every buck in the woods comes unglued. For roughly the next ten days, the big boys are real busy doing the job for which they were created. In a balanced herd, the little guys hang around the fringes hoping to get lucky. And then the peak of the rut is over. Buck movement drops like a stone. Small and medium-sized bucks give up on getting lucky and turn their attention to food. Hunters return home. It is over for another year.

But here is the good news. It's not really over. Yes, the craziness so often associated with the rut has ceased. But every big buck in the woods is still searching for that one last estrous doe. Big bucks, the breeder bucks, take their job very seriously. They don't give up just because the bulk of the does have been bred. Unlike the immature bucks, the mature bucks are not so quick to turn their attention to food. For them, the search for estrous does goes on. For you and I, that means that the waning rut provides us with one last chance for a really good buck.

I would not go so far as to say that I

Public land is a good bet during the waning rut. Odds are all of the other hunters have given up for another year and you will have it all to yourself.

prefer the waning rut over any other stage of the rut, but I will tell you that I do not miss out on it. Not ever. Somewhere, I'm hunting whitetail deer during the week of Thanksgiving. Three of my biggest bucks have fallen during the week of Thanksgiving. All three hang on my wall today because they were still actively seeking estrous does.

Two of the three came to the horns. Some of you might find that surprising, because, like me, you have read and heard time and again that the best time for rattling is prior to the actual commencement of breeding activities. That advice is sound. You will rattle in more bucks during the ten-day to two-week-long period leading up to the onset of actual breeding than you will during any other time. A lot of those bucks, however, will be immature bucks. On the back side of the rut, it is rare to have a small buck respond to rattling. This means that you will not see as much action, but the tradeoff is that the buck you do rattle up is likely to be a mature animal.

When I rattle up a buck prior to the breeding phase of the rut, that buck looks to me like he is looking for a fight.

Often, they have their ears laid back, the hair stands out on end to make them look even bigger and they walk with that sideways swagger. But a buck coming to the horns on the back side of the rut, looks to me like he is looking for a doe and trying to avoid a fight. I think most of the fight is out of them by now, but the urge to breed is not. I could be wrong, but that's the way it looks to me. Besides, it does not really matter why they come to the horns, the point is that they will. When I rattle on the back side of the rut, I am not as aggressive with the horns as I am earlier in the year. And even in really good areas, I do not expect to rattle up numbers of deer. I know that most of the bucks that hear the horns could care less. But there is one or two out there who still have the urge. That's what keeps me at it.

Calling is effective now too. Tending grunts are good, but I think that they are even more appealing to any buck within hearing if you mix in some doe bleats. Like I said, the bucks have lost some of their aggressiveness by this time, but they have not lost their sex drive. When they hear a doe

I don't expect to see a lot of action during the waning rut, but I'm never surprised when bucks like this show up either.

Sure, it can be cold. But it can heat up in a heartbeat.

bleat, they know that there is a doe in the picture. You can make authentic sounding doe bleats with a good variable tone grunt call. The True-Talker is my personal favorite because all it takes is a little finger pressure on the reed to go from a buck grunt to a doe bleat. Another option is a product called "The Can" from Primos. Turn it upside down and right it again and "The Can" emits a doe bleat. You can use "The Can" by itself or in harmony with a grunt tube.

As the fever pitch of peak rut subsides, little guys like this get back to eating, but the breeder bucks are still looking for one last hot doe.

If a buck does respond to your calling or rattling, a decoy will help you seal the deal. Remember, the buck that responds now is likely to be a mature buck. Odds are good he has been rattled up or called in before. A buck like that often demands visual confirmation before committing. Nothing provides that visual confirmation like a decoy.

Most of the time I like a buck decoy, but when hunting the waning rut I lean toward a doe decoy. A buck has only got one thing on his mind during this period and it is not a confrontation with another buck.

Laying down a scent trail with a drag rag saturated with doe-in-estrous urine is an excellent buck insurance policy when hunting the waning rut. When a buck is cruising for does, he spends a lot of time with his nose close to the ground. What he is doing is hoping to cut the track of a hot doe. If he smells a hot doe, he follows that scent trail to its source. For you skeptics out there, I will be the first to admit that a scent trail does not work all of the time. I have watched bucks step right over the scent trail I laid down without even giving it a cursory sniff. I've also watched them smell the scent trail and then just go on about their business. But some bucks, in fact most of the bucks I've seen cut the scent trail, have followed it. And perhaps most importantly, none have ever spooked from the scent trail. As I see it, you have everything to win and nothing to lose by laying down a scent trail as you walk into your stand.

As beneficial as rattling, calling, decoying and using scents can be, none of them will do you any good if you are not in the right spot. So, what is the right spot when hunting the waning rut? Hey, if I had a pat answer to that question, I would be the envy of every whitetail hunter in North America. I don't have a pat answer, but I can share with you what has worked best for me.

When hunting the dwindling days of the rut, think does, not bucks. It's all about the does now. Those big breeder bucks are going to spend their time checking out the places where does feed, bed and travel. During the mornings and midday, I like to hunt near known doe bedding areas or in travel corridors between two doe bedding areas. A travel corridor, which pinches down to form a natural funnel, is the best bet of all. In the evening, I like to situate myself near the food source that is attracting the most does. If the does are feeding in a field, I will usually hunt the edge of the field itself and use a decoy. Bucks often cruise back just

inside the cover and visually check the field for any sign of a doe. Without a decoy, many of these bucks will never stick their noses out of cover.

When I hunt the waning rut, I do not expect to be treated to wild rut action. I don't expect to see numbers of bucks. In fact, I am not surprised if I do not see a single buck. But I am not surprised either, when the buck I do see is the best buck of the season.

It ain't over until it is over.

Chapter Seven

The
ALL-DAY SIT

Don't ever kid yourself, there is nothing fun about sitting on a deer stand from dark to dark. So why do it, you might ask? Because in the world of whitetail hunting, there are very few guarantees, but this you can take to the bank: If you get in the habit of sitting all day in a good location when the rut is in progress, you will see more deer than you ever have before. Some of those deer will be bucks. One might be a real bomber.

I hunt whitetail deer from late August until late January each year. During those five months, I will spend nearly 100 days hunting deer. Out of those 100 days, I will average 30 days when I hunt all

A ground blind is much more comfortable than a tree stand when you are planning an all-day sit.

day. Hunting all day is hard work, so I choose the days when I sit all day with great care. Unless conditions are in my favor, I do not pull an all-day stint on stand. There are three conditions that will cause me to pull an all-day sit. One is hunting pressure, two is the approach of nasty weather and the third is the one we are most interested in here in this book, the rut. Hunting pressure means that deer might be on the move at any hour of the day. An approaching storm will nearly always see deer throwing caution to the wind and feeding heavily even at midday. And then there is my favorite time to pull an all-dayer. The rut. A roughly three-week-long period each fall when bucks spend all of their time making scrapes, rechecking those scrapes, destroying hapless saplings, fighting with other bucks, chasing does, breeding does and just generally making fools of themselves as they go about the business of procreation of the species. During the peak of the rut, it has been estimated that a mature buck is on his feet doing his thing for about 20 hours out of each 24-hour period. All of that daytime activity is what makes the rut my favorite time to stay put on a good stand all day.

I have written records of 30 years of deer hunting in personal journals. I didn't start keeping a journal of my hunts

Hunters will find that still-hunting is not simply a case of sitting comfortably under a tree all day.

with the idea of using it for research or for inclusion in books like this one, but my notes have turned out to be valuable in that regard. It will probably surprise no one that my records indicate the first two hours of shooting light to be the most productive period of the day in terms of bucks sighted on all-day sits during the rut. But it might surprise many hunters that the midday hours, specifically from 10:30 a.m. to 1:00 p.m., have accounted for almost twice as many

Cold drives more hunters from the stand prematurely than any other factor. The Heater Body Suit eliminates this problem.

buck sightings as have the heralded evening hours. I can't deliver a better argument for the all-day sit when the rut is on than that.

Where I hunt during the rut depends upon the stage of the rut. If the bucks are scraping and rubbing up a storm but the does are not yet interested in having anything to do with them, I spend my time sitting over the hottest rubs and

scrapes I can find. During this period I prefer to hunt over a decoy, al-ways use scents and I do a lot of rattling and calling. To me, this is the most exciting time of all to be in the woods. When the first does come into estrous, I abandon the scrapes and rubs and focus on the places frequented by does. I still use a decoy or two, make good use of doe-in-estrous scents and do a lot of rattling and calling.

Both mentally and physically, the all-day still-hunt can be a real challenge for most deer hunters. Boredom, fatigue and cold will conspire with doubt to drive you off your stand. If you make it one day, the next will be tougher, not easier.

Sure, just being out in the woods is pretty neat. Like you, I get a big kick out of watching squirrels and other critters. I like birds too. But trust me, even when there are birds and squirrels and even the occasional deer during the day, boredom is going to set in. Many hunters read a paperback book while on stand. Read a page, take a good look around, listen, then slowly turn to the next page. A good book will help pass the long uneventful hours. Some hunters wear earphones and listen to music or books on-tape. Some hunters even talk to friends or conduct business on their cell phones while on stand. I always bring a quality pair of binoculars. I've spent many enjoyable hours watching bobcat, fox, coyote, racoon, mink and even a timber wolf or two up close and personal through a good pair of binoculars. Oh yes, they work great for spotting deer too.

Doubt is the real killer. Once you begin to doubt that the place where you are sitting is the very best place where you can be sitting at that moment, you are in for a long, tough mental battle with yourself. Doubt will try to convince you that you should be down by the pasture or up on that next ridge.

There is only one way to defeat doubt. With confidence. The kind of confidence that comes through scouting and familiarity with the land you are hunting. That is why I find it nearly impossible to sit all day in a stand someone else has hung. That stand might well be smack-dab in the middle of a whitetail central. But I don't know it. Without confidence in your choice, doubt will win every time.

Fatigue tends to feed boredom and doubt. When I'm rested and mentally alert I can win those mental battles with my old foes boredom and doubt, but if I'm worn out from too many long days in the woods and not enough time in the sack, more often than not, they win. That is why I frequently take a little nap during the middle of the afternoon. When hunting from the ground, this is not much of a problem, but in a tree stand, napping can be a life-threatening activity. That is why I carry an extra safety belt in my fanny pack. I always wear a full harness with shoulder and leg straps when hunting from a tree stand, but I use the safety belt when I need to grab a nap. I wrap the safety belt around the tree and secure it tightly across my chest. With the safety belt secured, I don't tip forward each time I doze off and can grab a few winks. I don't sleep soundly and I don't sleep long, but even a 15-minute catnap can do wonders for my mental attitude and state of alertness for the rest of the day.

Food and drink are important when pulling an all-day sit. I've learned to pack more than I think I will eat. A couple of sandwiches, some cookies, dried fruit,

hard candy and a half-dozen sticks of jerky off of last year's buck. If the weather is on the warm side, I carry a jug of water but if it is cold, I carry a thermos of hot tea. My thermos happens to hold four small cups of tea. Often when the weather is cold, I play a little mind game with myself where a cup of tea is the reward for toughing it out another two hours—a cup of tea at ten, noon, two

and four. If that sounds ridiculous to you, then my guess is that you have never sat on a stand from dark to dark in cold weather. Of course, a lot of sane people have not!

Cold probably drives more hunters from their stands than any other factor. Living in Minnesota and doing much of my deer hunting in the northern states and Canadian provinces, I have spent a

Many good bucks move at midday. Maybe it is just coincidence that these are the same hours when most hunters have vacated the woods. Maybe not.

lot of time hunting in the cold. But I also make frequent trips south to hunt deer and I can tell you from experience that 20 above in the bone-chilling dampness of a Mississippi swamp feels colder than zero in Minnesota.

Staying put on stand in cold weather used to be a real torture test, but the cold is not the culprit it used to be. The cold weather hunting clothing, including boots, we have today is the best ever. Being a bit on the old-fashioned side, I have been told, I still rely primarily on wool for my outer layers for most of my hunting during the rut. With a layer or two of high-tech underwear underneath, a good pair of boots on my feet and warm hat snugged down on my head, I can stay surprisingly comfortable when hunting a few hours in the morning or evening, even when the bottom drops out of the old thermometer. But when I am planning to pull an "all-dayer" in cold conditions, I rely upon a Heater Body Suit. This insulated body suit works on the same principle as mittens. You know how mittens keep your hands warmer than gloves? The Heater Body Suit traps all of the heat trying to escape from your body and uses it to keep your body warm. Pretty slick. It rolls up into an easily backpacked six-pound bundle and slides off of your shoulders with ease when it is time for the shot. The Heater Body Suit comes in both a windproof and waterproof

Many hunters read a book to help pass the long hours. Read a page, look for deer, read another page.

model, but I prefer the windproof because it is very quiet. The small company that produces the Heater Body Suit is so confident that you will stay warm in their suit that they offer a very simple guarantee, "you stay warm or your money back."

Many hunters talk about pulling an all-dayer, but they never do. Others would not even entertain the idea. That's alright. It's not for everyone. But when the rut is on, no matter where in this country you hunt, if you can muster the physical and mental stamina to stick with it all day, you've just dramatically boosted your odds of getting a crack at a good buck.

Chapter Eight

ALTERNATIVES *to* STAND HUNTING

M ost of the time, hunting from a well-selected and correctly positioned tree stand or ground blind is the most effective method for hunting during the rut. When you hunt an animal with the finely tuned senses and often uncanny instincts for survival that a mature whitetail has at its disposal, you are nearly always better off letting that deer come to you. But as it is with every other aspect of hunting whitetail deer, there are exceptions to that rule and I would be remiss if I did not cover them in this book. So let's have a look at still-hunting, deer drives, tracking and spot and stalk, four alternatives to sitting on stand.

STILL-HUNTING

True still-hunting is nearly a lost art. Today, what most deer hunters call still-hunting is really nothing more than a walk in the woods. Effective still-hunting demands mega-doses of patience and self-restraint.

Still-hunting with a bow is not impossible; difficult for sure, but impossible it is not.

Still-hunting is not about covering ground or stretching the muscles after a long stint on stand. A good still-hunter might cover only a few yards in an hour. Still-hunters rely on their eyes and ears, not their legs. But even the best know that more often than not the deer will win the game. Even under the best conditions for still-hunting, when the forest floor is quiet from rain or wet snow, odds are that the deer will either see, hear or smell you before you can draw a bead on him. Still-hunting is the ultimate challenge in this game we call whitetail hunting.

The rut is a good time to be still-hunting because bucks are on the move now. Many would-be still-hunters make the mistake of attempting to still-hunt during periods when most of the deer are bedded down, but this is fool's folly. It is tough enough to get the drop on a deer that is on its feet. Slipping up within range of a bedded deer, which you do not even know is there, is a rare event.

I mentioned that conditions dictate whether or not still-hunting is even an option. If the ground is dry, forget still-hunting. You can't slip up on deer if you sound like a bowl of Rice Krispies with

Getting together with a partner, or a few buddies, to conduct a few well-organized deer drives is one alternative to stand hunting.

every step you take. Wind can help mask the sound, but I have found it to rarely be sufficient. But if the forest floor is wet from rain or snow, you can move quietly. Even a heavy frost will work. Just wait for it to melt in the morning. You usually have an hour or two before the leaves dry out and it becomes too noisy for still-hunting.

I also mentioned that good still-hunters do not cover much ground. The best example I can provide of that took place a few years ago in my home state of Minnesota, where the firearms deer season is held during the rut. A wet snow had fallen during the night and with that snow clinging to every branch and bush, the drab November timber of the previous day had been transformed into a dazzling, almost dizzying, world of white. I sat on my stand for the first hour or two and then gave in to the urge to still-hunt. I started my hunt along an aspen studded ridge that allowed me to move directly into the slight northerly breeze. The aspen here were thick and about as big around as a man's arm. I knew that does loved to bed down in those aspen and I knew that any buck looking for a little action would know it too. I had been slipping along for over an hour and had not covered the length of a football field. One or two cautious steps and then I would drop to a knee to scan under the snow laden branches in all directions. Look, listen, look again and then move another step or two. That is still-hunting.

Spot and stalk is a tactic not normally associated with whitetail deer, but there are places, predominately in the West, where this tactic can pay off for a good rifleman.

It was while on my right knee that I spotted the slender brown sapling. It was out of place in this world of white, but yet it did not immediately register. Then that sapling moved and so did three other similar saplings I had not seen. I could not see the deer's body or its head, but I knew it was a buck, because I had caught a glimpse of a large, bushy, black tarsal gland on the inside of one hind leg. The deer was only five or six yards away when

I first saw it and it was moving my way. I raised the old pump shotgun and waited. When the deer stepped into a small opening directly in front of me, I easily confirmed that it was indeed a buck and then mashed the trigger. The buck simply collapsed where he had stood. From the imprint of my knee in the snow to the fallen buck was a distance of seven feet, which means that the buck was probably no more than five feet from the business end of that twelve gauge. That buck is the only deer I have ever seen with powder burns on its hide.

DEER DRIVES

Deer drives, to my way of thinking, are a useful tool for getting deer to move when they are not moving on their own. But since the neat thing about hunting during the rut is that bucks are on the move, I personally rarely participate in a deer drive during the rut. Part of the reason for this is that I prefer to hunt for mature bucks and I learned early on that even during the rut, when a big buck is slightly addled by all of that testosterone, that such a deer will only rarely act the way drive participants expect him to act. Seven of us were hunting as a loosely knit group and when we met for a midday lunch after a morning on stand, one of the guys reported that he had seen a huge buck enter a small patch of heavy cover and not exit. This football-shaped tangle of red osier, scrub willow, canary grass and cattails was only about five acres in size and was completely surrounded by plowed ground. We positioned three hunters where they could cover all exits and then four of us started through that jungle. A doe broke on the first pass-through. We turned around and went back through it. This time one of my buddies nearly stepped on the mammoth buck. The buck exploded from literally under Petey's boots but before my startled friend could react the buck disappeared. Petey hollered "here he comes" so that the posters would be ready, but the buck never exited that cover. We went back through it again and then again. On our fifth pass, one of the guys jumped another buck from under his feet. Again the hunter could not get a shot, but the heavy eight-pointer crossed in front of me and I put him down. A nice buck, but not the big boy. We were all young and strong and determined, but that buck beat us. After a dozen or more passes through that small patch of heavy cover, we finally gave up and went back to our stands.

I've never forgotten the lesson that buck gave us. Sure, there are some good bucks killed on drives every year. But from what I have seen, it is a small percentage option. Big bucks don't panic like other deer. They have been through a drive or two in their day. They know how to react. Most of them, I am convinced, like that big buck in that slough, just hold their ground and

On a very windy day in Montana, a Realtree cameraman and I got down out of our tree stand and put a 500-yard sneak on a dandy ten-pointer.

let the drivers pass them by. The big ones are mighty cool customers.

Your best chance of killing a big buck on a deer drive during the rut is to catch that buck tending a doe and have the doe make a mistake. The buck will follow that doe anywhere—even to his death.

TRACKING

You need four conditions in your favor before you should ever consider tracking.

Fresh snow, lots of country, low deer density and few hunters. Obviously, you need the snow so that you can find and follow the tracks. Old snow is better than no snow, but it is difficult to stay on a fresh buck track when it is constantly intermingled with other deer tracks. Then too, unless you are really good, only a fresh snow provides evidence that the track you are on is really fresh.

Having the right snow conditions does

not do you much good if you only have a couple hundred acres to hunt on. A buck on the prowl can put on the miles in his search for does and you need unlimited public land or timber company land so that you can pretty much go wherever the buck goes.

In many regions of the country today, there are simply too many deer for tracking to be a viable option. Too many deer leave too many tracks and you end up spending most of your time trying to unravel the track you are on from all the others.

And then there is hunting pressure. If there are too many hunters, all you will end up doing is pushing the buck you are tracking right in to some other lucky hunter.

So as you can see, tracking is a technique that is very situation specific. It is also a tactic that calls for some serious stamina. Back in the days before Saskatchewan outfitters just stuck you in little wooden boxes for the day, I got on a big track one November morning just at first light. Deer density in the area I was hunting was one to three deer per square mile, so confusing his track with other deer tracks was not a problem. In fact, I saw more wolf and moose tracks than I did deer tracks. It was midafter-

Most hunters never consider slipping along a marsh edge or down a stream in a canoe or small boat. That is what makes this tactic so deadly.

noon and I had gone a long way and knew that I should give up and head back for the logging road where my truck was parked. But then I caught a glimpse of the buck. It was enough of a glimpse to make me want him real bad, so I made a poor decision and stayed on that track until it was so dark I could not see it anymore. Then I turned around and started back to the road. Two and a half hours later, all of it steady walking, put me there. That buck had taken me on quite a trip.

I've read about the exploits of the Benoits and those guys do it right, but the truth about tracking is that few hunters are going to encounter conditions conducive to good tracking and even fewer have what it takes to track down a big buck. If you ever do though, I will guarantee that, regardless of the headgear that buck is wearing, you will look upon that buck as one of your finest trophies.

SPOT AND STALK

Most of the places a whitetail calls home do not lend themselves well to the "spot" factor in spot and stalk. In fact, looking back over a lifetime of hunting whitetail deer, I suspect that at least half of the deer I have shot with a firearm were in range when I first saw them. But there are exceptions to every rule and so it is with spot and stalk for whitetail deer during the rut.

I am purposefully not including information on the dimunitive Coues deer here, because although technically a member of the whitetail clan, its range is so restricted and the number of hunters who pursue it so minimal, that I do not feel it fits the general theme of this book. However, if you ever have the chance to hunt for Coues deer, you will get your fill of spot and stalk hunting.

In the rest of the places the whitetail calls home, many spot and stalk opportunities are happenstance rather than planned. A half-dozen times I have spotted deer from my stand and then climbed down and attempted to stalk them. I've killed three bucks this way and while yes, I did spot them, and yes, I did stalk them, I do not consider this to be spot and stalk in the truest sense of the definition.

I know a number of very good hunters who cruise farm country roads during the rut looking for bucks tending does in agricultural areas. These hunters know that big bucks in farm country have learned that if they can push an estrous doe out into the wide-open farmland, they can avoid being pestered by rival bucks. I've seen bucks standing over does that have bedded down out in the middle of several hundred acres of soybean stubble, but more commonly you will find these farm country bucks using fence lines, drainage ditches, rock piles or whatever other skimpy cover exists. Good binoculars, a spotting scope and a heaping dose of patience once the stalk is undertaken are essential for this type of hunting. Try to rush the stalk in open

When the wind is blowing hard enough to rustle those cornstalks, sneak hunting a cornfield can be deadly during the rut.

farm country and you will get nailed every time. The old adage "just inching along" might well have been coined for just such an exercise. Slipping within gun range, especially a shotgun with slugs or a muzzleloader, which are usually required in farm country, is no easy feat. Slithering to within bow range is a near miracle.

Once, on the morning after a real doozy of a blizzard had dumped a foot of snow and sent temperatures plunging into that minus 20-degree range, I spotted a buck bedded down in a clump of cedars on a south-facing slope. He was soaking up what meager warmth the sun was generating that morning. Through the spotting scope I could see that he was contentedly chewing his cud and probably had no intention of vacating the place where he had weathered the storm until that evening. Some believe that deer are up and at it as soon as a major storm moves through, but that has not been my experience. Deer are perfectly content to forgo breakfast and conserve energy by staying put in their beds while they wait for the bitter northwest winds and brutal temperatures that normally fall on the heels of such storms to abate. Dressed totally in white, including my face mask and with my bow taped white as well, I moved slowly up the hill toward the bedded buck. The wind was in my favor and because it was blowing 20 mph or more, I did not have to worry about those fickle currents that will kill you in hill country. It took me over an hour but finally I belly crawled the last 50 yards to my objective, a snow-draped deadfall that I had estimated to be within 40 yards of the bedded buck. As it turned out, my estimate was off by ten yards and when I slipped the rangefinder from my pocket and zapped the buck, I was pleased to see that I was only 23 yards from the bedded buck. It was too cold to lay there and wait for the deer to stand up and move on its own and I was afraid if I grunted at the buck that he might bolt instead of just standing up and offering me a broadside shot. As I deliberated about taking the shot at the bedded buck, I saw an ear twitch. Only this ear was not attached to the buck's head. I dug my binoculars out from under my white fleece jacket and focused on where I had seen the ear twitch. Sure enough, there was a doe bed-ded just a yard or two to the left of the buck. I suspect that she was in heat. Now with another deer in the picture, I figured too many things could go wrong, so I drew while crouched down behind the scant cover of the deadfall, came to my knees, settled the pin and watched the arrow disappear right where I was aiming. If you are a bowhunter, you know what a good feeling that is. That buck is not the largest I have ever killed, but when it comes to memories, his will be one of the last to leave me.

Stand hunting is the most popular way to deer hunt. It should be, it is the deadliest of all tactics. But stand hunting is not the only method that works.

Chapter Nine

WEATHER
and the RUT

T he weather can make or break a hunt during the rut. That is why serious whitetail hunters are always glued to the Weather Channel and why a great many of them carry weather radios with them wherever they travel. Weather forecasts today are very good and knowing in advance what weather changes are in store for the next few days can greatly increase your odds of being in the right place at the right time. If I had the luxury, I would plan all of my hunts around the weather, but since neither I nor anyone I know is quite that fortunate, the best we can do is make the most out of whatever weather conditions we encounter.

In unseasonably warm weather, hunt near ponds and creeks where deer will come to drink.

HOT WEATHER

Nothing shuts down daytime rut activity quicker than unseasonably warm weather. It's not that bucks do not want to do their thing when the weather turns hot during the rut, it's just physically impossible for them to continue. Imagine running a marathon in mid-July while wearing long johns and a

There is not really much you can do about it either. Your best window of opportunity is the first hour of shooting light in the morning. Bucks that have been on the prowl during the night will continue to look for does until the sun is well up and the oppressive heat drives them to seek shade and comfort once again. Evenings

One thing about the weather and deer hunting that I do know for sure is if you are out in the places the deer call home, you always have a chance. If you stay in camp, you can forget it.

goose down coat. That's what a big buck all decked out in his own winter coat must feel like when he tries to go on about the business of procreation of the species when the weather turns hot. Does still get bred, but all of the activity takes place at night.

run a poor second to mornings when the weather is hot. Usually, it does not cool down significantly until well after dark, so bucks just lay in their beds, chew their cud and wait for the temperature to drop.

Exactly what constitutes unseasonably

warm temperatures will depend upon what part of the country you are hunting. A buck in central Alabama, for example, would be perfectly comfortable chasing does when the daytime temperature peaked in the mid-50s or even low 60s. But let a chinook wind blow in temperatures in that range across Saskatchewan, and I guarantee you that all daytime rutting activity will come to a sudden halt. I go by average seasonal temperature. If the temperature is above the seasonal average for the area you are hunting, you can figure on buck movement being diminished. A few degrees might not have much of an impact, but ten or more degrees will nearly always result in limited daytime buck movement.

If the heat is accompanied by high humidity, it is even worse. Rarely is this a problem in the northern states during the rut, but in the South, the combination of heat and humidity can literally put a stop to buck movement. Years ago, shortly after Bill Jordan introduced his now insanely popular Realtree camouflage, I used to hunt with him on some property that he leased not far from Columbus, Georgia. There was a power line right-of-way that dissected the property and Bill had several stands hung at major crossings on that right-of-way. Since you could see a long way in both directions from the stand, it was not unusual to see 50 or more deer cross the right-of-way in a morning or evening on stand and several times I counted over 100 deer in a single sit.

On one hunt, which took place during the first few days of the rut in that area, I sat on stands overlooking that power line as the temperature and humidity soared to summertime levels. For two days the heat persisted. My journal indicates that I saw six does on the first morning of hot, humid weather and only a lone doe and fawn that evening. The following morning, I saw three does and fawns and that evening, I never saw a single deer. Up until that experience, I would have gladly bet you my house that it was impossible to sit on any of those stands during the first or last hours of light and not see a single deer.

By the way, my journal also reminds me that a nasty thunderstorm, with some of the loudest thunder I have ever heard, hammered away most of the night after the second straight day of uncommon heat. In the morning, Bill and I crossed swollen creeks that nearly washed away the old, brown Suburban we called the "team bus." The day before we had crossed the same creeks without getting the tires wet. The rain had subsided about an hour before first light. The rain had cooled things off considerably, but now on the back side of the storm, you could feel the temperature rapidly dropping even lower. I saw 47 deer that morning, nine of them bucks. Bill, I am sure would have seen just as many, had he not dropped a dandy ten-pointer as it chased a doe past his stand right at first light.

When faced with unseasonably warm

weather-stay abreast of the forecast. When the forecasters predict a change in the weather, be in the woods.

Well-organized deer drives are another option in hot weather. Normally, I do not like to do any driving during the rut. Drives are disruptive to natural rut-induced movement and I do not want to do anything to disrupt the natural buck movement. But when the weather is unseasonably warm, drives are an option. The problem, of course, is that who wants to be out tromping through the timber when it is uncomfortably hot just sitting in the shade. I've participated in a few of these warm weather drives and invariably after only one or two drives, everyone is ready to call it a day.

RAIN

Even a hard, fall rain, the kind my buddies in the South call a real "Georgia frog choker," won't bring rutting activity to a standstill the way that oppressive heat will, but it will darn sure put a damper on it, no pun intended. I don't like hunting in a hard rain, but I've done it often enough to know that if the rut is in full swing, some bucks might still be on the move. Bowhunting in my home state one November during the peak of the rut, I had to keep the windshield wipers on high speed as I drove to my hunting area. When I finally got to where I was going, I sat in the pickup, with the radio volume cranked up high so that I could hear the weather forecast over the insane pounding of the

rain on the cab: "Rain continuing through the morning hours, accumulations of three to five inches, before turning to sleet, freezing rain or snow by late afternoon." I'll admit that I gave some thought to turning around and going home. But the rut only comes once a year where I live, so I pulled on rain gear over my warm clothes, grabbed my bow and headed for a gnarly old oak where I had hung a stand a week or two prior to my hunt. By 8 o'clock I was miserable. An hour later I told myself I was insane. By 10 o'clock I promised myself just one more hour. Just before noon, after breaking the promise I had made to myself at 10 o'clock, I saw my first deer. It was a doe and although she looked to be as miserable, wet and cold as I was, she also had that look about her that told me she was in heat. When a minute later, a small eight-point buck emerged from the same tangle the doe had exited, I knew I had been right in my assessment. Then another slightly larger buck appeared. Then King Kong! He was a monster whitetail. When he stopped 40 yards away to shake the water from his coat, the spray flew six feet in all directions. I was already shaking from being cold and wet. Now I really started to shake. At first it looked like I was going to get a crack at the big boy right away, but then the doe turned away and simply bedded down at the edge of the timber 60 yards from where I perched. The big buck spent the next four hours standing near her. Each time one of the two smaller

It was 27 degrees below zero the November morning I rattled in this big Saskatchewan buck. Always remember, what we humans think is brutal weather might be nothing to a whitetail.

bucks would get too close, the big boy would put the run on them, usually by simply posturing. The younger bucks seemed to know their place, but just could not give up hope. Each of the young bucks walked under my tree numerous times that afternoon, but the big boy never left the doe. Finally, late in the afternoon, as the rain, as the weatherman had promised, turned to a mixture of stinging sleet and wet, sloppy slush, the doe got to her feet and headed in my direction. The big buck was right on her tail.

By now, I was shaking uncontrollably and most of it had nothing to do with the deer. This was back in the early days of Gore-Tex rain gear and the new outfit I was wearing on that hunt, like many of that first generation, had not been sealed properly. I was soaked to the skin and had been for many hours. I knew that I was flirting with hypothermia, but I just could not bring myself to climb down while that big buck was hanging around.

The doe walked past on a trail just 22 steps from the base of my tree. When I tried to draw, I could not get the 73-pound Mathews back. The buck kept walking. I let down and summoning everything I had, I jerked that string back and tried without success to control my muscles long enough to steady the pin somewhere behind the buck's near shoulder. I could not and when I finally just let the string go, I missed the buck by a foot and a half.

In general, intensity and longevity determine what effect rain will have on buck movement during the rut. There is no question that a hard, persistent rain will lead to a decrease in deer movement. Most deer will seek the best overhead cover the area has to offer, most commonly conifers, and stay put until the rain slacks off. But a hard rain that does not last long, what is commonly referred to as a "passing shower," will not have any adverse affect on buck movement during the rut. In fact, if the shower occurs during warmer than normal weather, the rain may spur buck movement both during the shower and afterward.

Light rain, or what we call a "drizzle" in my part of the country, is quite common during the rut. I look forward to hunting on such days. Buck movement can be exceptional when a light rain or drizzle is falling. I do not know if this is because the temperature is to their liking when a light rain is falling, or if it has to do with the low light common to such days. My guess is that it is probably a combination of these

In the midwestern snow, cold and corn all go together. When the weather turns cold, deer turn their attention to corn.

two factors and possibly others that we humans will never understand. The "why" is not really important to me anyway. It is enough for me just to know that a day with light rain or drizzle has nearly always resulted in multiple buck sightings when hunting during the rut. And like many others who spend much of the rut shaking a set of rattling antlers, I have found that bucks tend to be especially susceptible to the "horns" on such days.

Allow me to include fog in with this discussion of rain, because it has been my experience that fog, like drizzle, promotes good buck movement during the rut. I dislike hunting in thick fog for the obvious reason that you cannot see the deer and for the less obvious reason that I have several times become hopelessly turned around while attempting to locate my stand on such mornings. One time while hunting not far from the Mississippi River in the beautiful bluff country of Wisconsin's famed Buffalo County, the morning fog was so thick that the Army Corps of Engineers had halted all barge traffic on the river. I, of course, should not have been risking my life making the 80-mile drive from my home to the little farm I lease back in the hills high above the river, but somehow whatever admittedly small portion of good, common sense I possess at other times of the year seems to vacate me completely when the rut is in progress. I left home an hour early, because I knew that it was going to be a long slow drive and arrived at the farm before first light. Like I said, the farm is small, only about 100 acres and I have hunted if for a number of years, so there is not an inch of it I do not know. I was certain when I left the pickup that I could hike directly across the small alfalfa field, drop down into the valley, cross the creek and find my stand on the ridge above the creek. An hour later I had crossed the creek four times. Finally, I had to admit that I had no idea where I was, so I sat down with my back against a tree and waited for the fog to lift. The fog was especially stubborn that morning, and it was several hours before it began to burn off. When it did, I began to look around me for any familiar landmarks. Through the fog, I spotted one. It was my pickup!

But there is fog and then there is fog. I've learned my lesson. Some fog is just too thick to hunt in. Deer may move in it, I don't know. But it really does not matter when you can't see the broadhead on the end of your arrow. But a light fog is a different matter. I think deer movement increases when a light fog cloaks the land. It is one of my favorite times to be working a set of rattling antlers. On Giles Island one foggy morning I rattled up nine different bucks before breakfast. On clear days during the rut on the same island, I have rattled all day and not brought a single buck to the horns. On another memorable morning while hunting the Encinido's Ranch in South Texas with my friend John Pflueger during the mid-December rutting period, we rattled up 13 bucks one morning before the morning ground fog wore off. The rest of the day, we rattled in zero. The next morning, with the ground fog once again casting its palor over the mesquite and prickly pear, a very nice ten-pointer came to the horns at our first set of the morning. I shot him, which ruined what otherwise might well have been another exceptional day of rattling action.

Snow and cold are a deer hunter's friends. No more guessing where the deer bed or where they are feeding.

SNOW

Born and raised in the north country, I am partial to snow. Anytime I can hunt big whitetail bucks during the rut and have snow on the ground to boot, I am one happy camper. Snow makes deer easier to see. And when there is snow on the ground, scouting is a simple task. The tracks and trails tell you where the deer are traveling. Scrapes show up against the snow like big zits on a pretty girl's face.

I don't know if deer "like" snow or not, but I know that they are very active when it is snowing, especially during those first snowfalls of the year, which luckily for us often occur about the time of the rut.

Of course, you can have too much of a good thing, even snow. I have hunted in conditions where so much snow fell in such a short period of time that deer simply laid low and let the storm pass. Even after the snow had quit falling, the snow on the ground was so deep that it took the deer a day or two to adjust and develop patterns. In each case, however, these were late season situations. It would be very unusual to have snow in that quantity during the rut, although it is possible for those who hunt the Canadian provinces or the northern extremes of states such as Minnesota, Michigan, Wisconsin, Montana, Maine, Vermont and New York.

COLD

The whitetail deer is well suited for handling cold weather. Thinking back over a lifetime spent hunting deer, I cannot recall a single instance when the weather got so cold during the rut that it shut down daytime rutting activity. I can, however, easily recall a couple of dozen instances when a cold front ushered in not only cold temperatures, low humidity and high pressure but some of the best rut action I've ever experienced.

The first time I ever hunted Saskatchewan, I made the mistake of opting to hunt the last ten days of October. I had a great time, met some good people with whom I am friends to this day and learned that the big bucks in the northern reaches of this province don't even think about getting cranked up for the rut until the last few days of October. The only mature deer I saw were three big bucks still traveling together on Halloween morning just before I had to leave to catch a plane back home. In mid-November I drove back up to Saskatchewan hoping to get a crack at one of those three big bucks I had seen on Halloween. One of those warm westerly winds they call a "chinook" had blown in the day before I arrived and the warm spell hung on for three or four days. Deer movement was at a standstill. But then one night, the wind switched to the northwest, a few inches of snow fell and the temperature dropped quicker than the stock market. When I climbed into my tree stand the next morning it was 27 degrees below zero. Shortly after noon that day, when the biggest buck I have ever killed came to the sound of my rattling antlers, it had warmed up to minus 15 degrees. I can't be 100 percent certain, but I believe that the buck I killed that cold day was the second largest of the three bucks I had seen traveling together on the last day of October.

With only one day left to hunt, I drove to the nearest town and plunked down $268 American for another deer tag. At that time, nonresident aliens (that's us) could take two deer per season in Saskatchewan. That law has since been changed and we are now limited to one buck per season. I remember my outfitter, a young man named Mick Manson, just shaking his head as I counted out the dollars for the license on the counter of the little store. "It takes you two trips and sixteen days of hunting to kill one buck and now you are willing to risk $268 on the slim hope that you can kill another in just one day?" he questioned only half jokingly.

"The time is right Mick," I replied. "This cold snap has tripped the trigger. These bucks are on the move big time. I would never forgive myself if I went home and did not give it that last day."

As it turned out, it was the best $268 I have ever spent. The next morning, with the temperature still well below zero and every twig and branch in the forest covered with hoarfrost, another of those oversized brutes for which Saskatchewan is famous came to the ancient clatter of antler on antler.

If you are a serious whitetail hunter, cold weather during the rut is your friend, not your enemy.

WIND

There are those who claim that deer do not move well when the wind gets to blowing. I've had some hunters tell me that 15 is the magic number. Anytime the wind is blowing at 15 miles per hour or better, these hunters say deer movement is greatly curtailed. Others have told me that 20 or 25 miles per hour is the magic number. Maybe these numbers have some validity when the rut is not in progress. But I can tell you from plenty of personal experience with hunting in the wind that a buck supercharged on straight testosterone is only concerned about one thing, and it is not the wind.

On the Milk River in Montana one Halloween evening, I killed a 150-inch ten-pointer in a little Montana breeze that was officially clocked in excess of 90 miles per hour. Realtree cameraman Mark Womack and I had been trying to hunt from a tree stand hung in a gnarly old river bottom cottonwood that was big enough around the trunk that two men could not touch fingertips if they reached around that tree from opposite sides. But even before the wind had reached its peak, that stout cottonwood was swaying so wildly that filming from it was impossible. When the ten-pointer walked out of the river bottom timber a quarter-mile away and began working a string of scrapes along the edge of an alfalfa field, Mark and I climbed down, put a stalk on the buck and managed to take him on camera. Someone had forgotten to tell that buck and the 30 or so other deer we saw that evening that it was too windy for them to be out and about.

In Nebraska, another state with a well-deserved reputation for being a bit on the breezy side, I had a stout eight-pointer coming into my decoy one windy afternoon. That buck, like so many I have seen, was ready to take out my old faithful fake. The buck had his ears laid back and the hair on his entire body stood on end to make him look even bigger and badder than he really was. I had my release on the string, my feet in position and was muttering my mantra, pick a spot, pick a spot, pick a spot, when an especially violent gust of wind toppled my decoy. The buck stopped in mid-stride and just stared at the fallen decoy for what seemed like a long time, then he turned and walked away. Sure, the wind got me that afternoon but not because the deer were not moving.

WATCH THAT BAROMETER

Like many other serious whitetail hunters, I keep a close eye on the barometer. Deer movement during the rut or at any other time seems to spike when the barometer is on the move. In my experience, a falling barometer will spur deer movement, but not nearly as much as will a rising barometer.

I am convinced, as are many others, that many birds and animals have built-in weather forecasting systems. I don't know how it works. Nobody does. But many critters, whitetail deer included, react to changes in the weather before we ever experience the weather change. Sometimes they react a day or two in advance. We should too.

The wind was blowing 93 miles per hour when I shot this ten-point buck as he checked a string of scrapes. According to everything I have read, no deer should have been out and about in a gale like that, but I guess this buck did not know any better—and neither did I!

Chapter Ten

HOW *to* BEAT *the* BIG STINK

Many hunters are convinced that the only way to go undetected by a whitetail's sense of smell is to make sure that the deer never get downwind of their position. That's a great theory, but it is not really practical. Very few stand locations force deer to remain upwind of the stand. You don't have to hunt deer very long before you realize that deer are forever showing up where you least expect to see them. Many times, this means downwind. And even if you play the wind, you can't trust it. The wind is forever shifting. It might be dead in your face when you climb into your stand, on your right cheek an hour later and on your left cheek before noon. What are you going to do, change stands each time the wind shifts?

I think odor control is more important today than it was 20 or 30 years

The single most important change I have made in my deer hunting strategy has been to implement a complete odor control program.

ago, just because of the sheer numbers of deer. The more deer there are, the better the odds that some of those deer are going to get downwind of your position.

I have practiced serious odor control for many years, but I would never go so far as to say that it is possible to be 100 percent odor free. It is not. But what you can do is control human odor to the extent that deer will be less likely to smell you. This is a huge advantage. In fact, I consider serious odor control to be the most important advancement I have made in my own hunting strategy in the last 20 years.

I guess that is why I am constantly amazed at hunters today who scoff at the

I keep all of my clothing in scent-safe bags and spray them down before each hunt with a good odor neutralizer.

whole idea of odor control. In the high tech world we live in today, how can it be so difficult to believe that there are products at our disposal that will greatly eliminate the amount of human scent we give off in the woods?

Yes, there have certainly been some unscrupulous manufacturers in the odor control business. They have attempted to sell us products that did not do what they claimed. But deer hunters are not a bunch of dummies. We caught on. Word of mouth advertising works both ways you know. Gimmicks don't last long. We are very fortunate today to have a host of products available to us that actually do exactly what the manufactures claim they will do. In fact, the number of legitimate tools you and I can use to minimize our human odor is constantly expanding while those that have stood the test of time are being refined and improved upon.

You and I will never completely understand the whitetail deer's sense of smell. It is too complex, too finely tuned. It is the sense that has allowed the whitetail to survive for all of these centuries. Sure, a whitetail has good eyes. Hearing too. But it is that incredible sense of smell upon which the whitetail relies most heavily. A whitetail's nose does much more than serve as an early warning system. That black nose helps a whitetail locate food and water, find a hot doe, identify other deer and read a thousand other messages carried on the breeze, which you and I will never be able to decipher.

Looking back, I can see that I have been concerned with odor control for most of my hunting career. For years, I hung my hunting clothes outside where they could freshen in the air. Later, I started storing my outerwear with leaves, dirt or pine needles, letting the fabric absorb the

A little odor eliminating powder inside of the boots before each hunt goes a long way toward eliminating foot odor.

stopped for a bite on the way home from hunting one evening and forgot about the essence of skunk I had liberally poured on my boots.

Sometime in the early 1980s, I began to use odor reducing sprays and powders and that is when I really got serious about odor control. When Scent-Lok introduced that first green suit with something they called activated charcoal in 1990, I was one of the first hunters in this nation to be wearing one.

Today, I have an odor control program that I try to follow each time I go hunting. I consider this attention to odor control the single greatest advancement I have made in my hunting strategy over the past 20 years. I know that paying attention to odor control has allowed me to see more deer, have better shots at deer at close range and take more big bucks. You will probably come up with your own regimen for odor control. I share mine with you here to give you a platform from which to begin.

smells of the earth. I have even gone so far as to bury my hunting clothing in the garden for a week or two before the season, letting the fabric soak up those "earthy" odors. And I guess I've used about every cover scent ever invented at one time or another. I doubt that I will ever forget the look on the faces of the other folks in the restaurant the time I

ONE: Shower with a scent-free soap and shampoo before each hunt whenever possible. If you cannot shower, use Scent-A-Way wash towels for a PT&A bath.

TWO: Use a scent-free antiperspirant. If you use a powder, make sure it is unscented.

THREE: Dress in clothing that has been washed in an odor-free laundry soap and stored in a scent-safe bag or an airtight container. This should include underwear and socks.

FOUR: Sprinkle an odor eliminating powder in your boots and rub some in the sweat-band of your cap.

FIVE: Wear an activated charcoal suit including the hood or face mask. I know that many hunters, myself included, do not like hoods, but I've proven to myself many times that if you do not wear the hood, you cut the effectiveness of the suit in half. I try to put on my Scent-Lok suit after I arrive at my destination. If I have a long hike into my stand, I often carry my Scent-Lok suit in with me and stop about 100 yards before I get to my stand to put the suit on.

SIX: Spray down your outer layer of clothing and all of your gear with an odor eliminating spray before getting into your stand and repeat every few hours while on stand.

Just a few of the many odor eliminating products available today.

GETTING THE MOST OUT OF YOUR SCENT-LOK SUIT

Hunting clothing with activated charcoal for controlling human odor is a major investment for most of us. Whether you purchase the original Scent-Lok garments, clothing made with W.L. Gore's Suprescent or an outfit featuring Scent-Tek from Robinson Labs, you can figure on paying anywhere from $150 up to $500 for a complete set of activated charcoal clothing. Take care of your activated

Spray your boots down with an odor neutralizer before each hunt and it does not matter if you wear leather or rubber boots, you will not be leaving scent behind.

in-the-field experience. But before we get into how you can make sure that your garments are doing the job for you every time you put them on and how you can wring the most mileage possible out of your activated charcoal clothing, it is important to understand how activated charcoal works to help control human odor.

A layer of activated charcoal, the best of which is made from coconut hulls, is sandwiched between two layers of fabric. Just as the filter on your furnace captures and holds dust and debris that otherwise would be spread around your home, activated charcoal, through a process called adsorption, traps and holds the scent molecules that make you and I stink to whitetail deer and other critters with equally sensitive senses of smell. This process is no gimmick. Activated charcoal has been used in many industrial applications and by the military for many years. Greg Sesselmann and George Schrink, a couple of engineers with expertise in the aerospace carbon filtration field, founded Scent-Lok in the early '90s because they envisioned an application for activated charcoal technology in the hunting

charcoal garments and they will serve you well for many years.

I've been wearing activated charcoal garments while hunting whitetail deer and other big game since 1990, the year before Scent-Lok first introduced their original green liner to the hunting world. Since then, I've averaged 75 days each season wearing activated charcoal clothing. That does not make me an expert on activated charcoal, but it has provided me with some

world. The rest, as they say, is history.

Look at activated charcoal under a microscope and you will see that each particle is a maze of nooks, crannies and crevices. It is within these nooks and crannies that the gunk that makes you and I stink is trapped and held so that it cannot reach the atmosphere. Naturally, once the nooks and crannies are full, the activated charcoal can no longer do its job. To "cleanse" the activated charcoal, you reactivate it with heat. Heat causes the activated charcoal to purge itself. The problem here is that it takes at least 800 degrees for complete reactivation, a temperature you cannot attain without burning up the suit itself. You can, however, partially restore the activated charcoal by putting the suit into a clothes dryer on its hottest setting for 45 minutes. Before placing my suit in a dryer, I always spray down the interior of the dryer with an odor eliminator to eliminate any foreign odors.

When I take my suit out of the dryer, I roll it up tightly and place it in a Scent Safe clothing bag from H.S. Scents. Do not use a standard garbage bag. The plastic used in garbage bags has a distinctive odor and this odor will be transferred to your clothing. The Scent Safe bag goes inside of one of those green Scent-Safe Travel bags. This double protection ensures that my activated charcoal garments will not be subjected to any foreign odors prior to my hunt.

Usually, I drive to my hunting area wearing an old pair of sweats and dress in my activated charcoal garments on the tailgate of my truck when I arrive at my destination. This ensures that I will not contaminate my clothing with odors from the house or camp, from any stops along the way for food or fuel, or with odors from the vehicle itself. The most common mistake I see hunters make when it comes to activated charcoal clothing is getting dressed at home or in camp and then driving to the hunting area. When I am done

Big deer live and die by their noses.

hunting for the day, my activated charcoal garments come off when I get back to my vehicle and are stored in the odor-free double-bag system again. This dressing and undressing at the vehicle is admittedly a hassle, but it is worth the effort.

One of the questions I am most frequently asked regarding activated charcoal garments is how often should they be reactivated? Unfortunately, there is no pat answer to that question because there are too many variables to be considered. One variable is that each of us is an individual when it comes to how much odor we give off. Put simply, some of us stink more than others. Naturally, if you are one of those who is on the high end of the stink spectrum, you will need to reactivate more often than someone on the low end. The second variable that must be considered is the weather. In warm weather we tend to sweat and thus stink more than we do in cold weather. And the third variable is the activated charcoal garment itself. Today there are dozens of choices out there. Garments designed for warm weather sometimes have less activated charcoal sandwiched between the two layers of fabric than do garments designed for hunting in colder weather. Naturally, the less activated charcoal you have working for you, the more often you will need to reactivate. My advice is when in doubt reactivate. You cannot "wear out" the activated charcoal by frequent reactivation. Personally, I throw mine in the dryer after about every

30 hours of hunting.

For many years, washing activated charcoal garments was not recommended. However, that has all changed and you can now wash your activated charcoal garments as often as you like with no fear of decreasing the effectiveness of the activated charcoal itself and you may even enhance its ability to do it's job. Use a detergent that is specially formulated for activated charcoal garments or rely upon Atsko Sport-Wash that does not leave behind any odor or soap residue.

If you care for your activated charcoal garments, they will do their job for you for a long, long time.

NOT JUST FOR BOWHUNTERS

Although bowhunters were the first to embrace activated charcoal clothing and still account for the bulk of sales, those who hunt deer with firearms are slowly beginning to realize that controlling their human odor will lead to seeing more deer, having better shots at close-range deer and that it is the most important step they can take to improving their odds of drawing a bead on a real bruiser of a buck.

Personally, I do a lot of deer hunting with a muzzleloader, and I cannot remember the last time in the last ten years that I entered the woods carrying my smokepole without a layer of activated charcoal between my hide and the whitetail's nose. Those who hunt with shotguns and slugs also need deer to be reasonably close for a clean kill and will benefit greatly from using activated charcoal. But I believe that even those who hunt with centerfire rifles, which in the hands of a competent rifleman are deadly at long range, can benefit from activated charcoal technology. Most of the deer killed in North America, regardless of the type of firearm used, are taken at well under 100 yards.

Every deer hunter with a few seasons under his or her belt has experienced the frustration of having a deer blowing and snorting in alarm as it picks up the hunter's scent. But for every deer that we see spook or hear snort, there are probably two or three others that simply detect our presence with their sense of smell and take evasive action to avoid us. Wearing an activated charcoal suit will dramatically decrease these instances.

I actually had deer eating hay off of this haybale blind while I was inside. You can't do that without odor control.

Chapter Eleven

PRIME-TIME RATTLING

I have been fortunate enough to travel extensively in the pursuit of my favorite big game animal, the whitetail deer. Wherever I go, if the rut is on, my rattling antlers go with me. I've had bucks come to rattling in a bunch of states and provinces and while I have gotten over the "wow this stuff really does work," the adrenalin rush that jolts my system when a buck comes to the horns is still with me. Rattling in a buck is pure excitement. That's why I think it is sad that most whitetail hunters have never rattled in a buck. Many have tried, become discouraged and given up. Others have never even tried. Most are convinced that rattling is something that only works on the exclusive ranches in South Texas or some other exotic location. When I give whitetail seminars on rattling, no matter what

Some hunters like to slam those horns together; others, like me, are "grinders." It probably does not matter to the deer. Just do what feels good and stick with it.

The most bucks I have ever rattled up in a single morning was on a foggy morning just like this one, when thirteen different bucks (and a lone doe) came to the horns.

part of the country I am in, the most frequent comment I hear is "rattlin' don't work around here." With that attitude, these hunters are right, rattling never will work for them. But after several decades of horn shaking all across North America, I am convinced that rattling will work to some degree wherever there exists a population of whitetail deer.

In the world of real estate, location is everything. Many hunters believe that location is also the key to rattling success. If you happen to be fortunate enough to be hunting a ranch in South Texas or maybe the deep forest of northern Saskatchewan, then rattling might just work, these hunters figure. But if you are stuck with hunting Missouri, Alabama, New York, New Jersey, Wisconsin or Pennsylvania, for example, forget it. The truth is that location has nothing to do with how successful you will be in rattling up bucks. A southern buck is as susceptible to rattling as a northern buck and a buck in the East is just as likely to come to the horns as a western prairie whitetail. Nope, latitude and longitude have nothing to do with it, but the buck-to-doe ratio sure as heck does.

The reason why South Texas has developed a reputation as the horn-shaking mecca of the world is because 99.9 percent of the whitetail habitat in South Texas is under private ownership, the bulk of it in the form of large ranches. Whitetail deer are managed as a cash crop on many of these ranches. Each mature buck is worth a lot of cash. Hunters of means are willing to pay big bucks for a chance at a big buck. To ensure that the land is carrying the optimum number of mature bucks, the deer herds are intensely managed in an effort to keep the buck-to-doe ratio as close to one-to-one as possible. Of course, achieving such a perfect balance is nearly impossible, but ratios of one-to-two or one-to-three are common on these ranches. When you have a whitetail herd comprised of one adult buck for every two or three adult does, you are going to have competition between the bucks for breeding rights and anytime you have competition between bucks, rattling is a very effective technique. If the buck-to-doe ratio is out of whack, as it is in many parts of the country today, there is little or no competition between bucks for breeding rights because every buck has all of the does he can handle and then some.

Naturally, I look forward to the few opportunities I have to hunt in places where the buck-to-doe ratio is low enough to guarantee competition be-tween mature bucks. But most of the 70 to 90 days I spend hunting deer each season are spent in places where the buck-to-doe ratio tips heavily in favor of the does. Yet I have rattled in bucks in many of these less-than-ideal locations. Why? Curiosity is part of the reason. Whitetail deer are curious critters. When a buck hears what he believes to be two other bucks fighting, pure curiosity will sometimes trip his trigger. I believe this also explains why it is not uncommon to have does come to investigate the sound of rattling antlers.

Timing is critical when it comes to rattling success. Sure, you might rattle in a buck at anytime during the season, but your odds go way up when you present your case during the period when bucks are most likely to respond to your invitation. The exact dates will vary by region and somewhat from year to year, but the prime period for rattling action is that ten-day to two-week-long stretch leading up to the first wave of does entering estrous. Anywhere in the country where the annual rut is a relatively short, well-defined event, this is the time period when you want to be shaking those horns every chance you get. This is the stretch during which bucks are gearing up for the big event. Bucks are now on their feet a good share of each 24 hours as they paw out scrapes, make rubs and roam from doe group to doe group in the hope of encountering a ready doe. At the beginning of this period, most bucks that come to the horns will come in slow and wary. But during those last frantic days, when a buck is beside himself with pent-up frustration,

I've seen them literally charge in. It is quite a sight to see a mature buck come crashing through the brush and then come skidding to a halt right in front of you. Unnerving is a good word for it I think.

Once actual breeding commences, rattling success will vary greatly depending upon herd composition where you are hunting. If you are hunting in an area where does greatly outnumber bucks, the odds of rattling up a buck during peak rut are slim, simply because the buck is going to be so busy with one doe right after the other, that he has little time or inclination to respond to rattling. But if you are fortunate enough to be hunting a place where the buck-to-doe ratio is not out of whack, rattling during peak rut can bring surprisingly good results. If a buck is between hot does, which will often be the case in regions where the buck-to-doe ratio is not tilted heavily in favor of the does, that buck is a sucker for rattling during peak rut. After all, most buck battles during peak rut are fought over a doe. Bucks know this. Why not scoot on over there and see if maybe you can't steal that little gal away while the other two duke it out?

And then there is the downside of the rut, or what I call the "waning rut." You won't rattle up many bucks during this period, but the ones that do respond are likely to be the largest bucks in the area. The big boys are the last to give up on finding one more estrous doe.

It should go without saying that rattling

This South Texas ten-pointer came to the horns just at sunrise one mid-December morning. South Texas and rattling are synonymous, but even though the rattling is better here than anywhere I have hunted, it is not the only place where rattling works.

up a buck where you have no chance of getting a good shot at the buck is a waste of time and effort, but I've seen hunters do it many times. When bowhunting, where I need that buck within 30 yards or less, I like to do my rattling from a tree stand located in heavy cover. The reason I choose heavy cover when rattling while bowhunting is that a buck does not expect to be able to see the bucks he hears fighting until he is right on top of them when he is in heavy cover, so he is less likely to hang up. That is the plus side of

rattling from heavy cover. The downside is that bucks have this irritating habit of circling in downwind before committing themselves. In fact, during a recent three-year study on rattling conducted in South Texas where one team was on the ground rattling while another team was in an observation tower where they could easily see the rattling team and any deer that responded to the rattling, 60 percent of the bucks that responded came in from downwind. When they pull that maneuver in heavy cover, they rarely offer you a

This hunter is using a round bale for cover while rattling. Bringing a buck across the field won't be easy, but bringing one to the edge of the field is no problem.

When I'm gun hunting and can reach out there and touch them at 100 yards or more, I figure what the heck, go ahead and let them hang up! Now I hunt semi-open habitat.

Let your weapon determine the cover from which you do your rattling.

HOW TO RATTLE

No two buck fights ever sound the same, so it is not important how you choose to work your rattling antlers. When on the ground, many hunters like to rake brush and pound the ground while working the horns. I do too sometimes. Other hunters like to grunt, either by mouth or with a grunt call at the same time as they rattle. The truth is, you can go ahead and make all the racket you can muster and you will still never be able to duplicate the noise two mature bucks make when they are really getting it on. I know this: When I finish a rattling session, I am physically tired. If you are really getting it on with the horns, you will be too. That rattling study done down in Texas confirms this. The researchers rattled both soft and hard. During 86 soft rattling sessions, 30 bucks responded. But when the researchers cranked up the volume, 85 sequences resulted in 81 bucks coming to the horns. Now granted, you and I are not going to get that kind of response rate where we hunt, but the numbers do speak for themselves on this subject.

shot. To remedy this problem, try to set up with a large opening, a river, steep bank or something else at your back where deer will be reluctant to cross or enter. This will encourage them to circle in front of you instead of behind you.

If you use a decoy while bowhunting, forget everything I just said about heavy cover. When using a decoy, you need that decoy to be in the open where the deer can see it. We will cover this in detail in the chapter on decoying, so I won't go into it here.

In my experience, most hunters don't rattle long enough. Keep it up for at least a minute or two. I often rattle for five to seven minutes at a stretch, pausing about every 30 seconds to look and listen for approaching bucks. Longer rattling sessions have the advantage of giving the buck that hears the rattling time to make up his mind whether or not he wants to respond and then make the trip. Stay put for at least 30 minutes. Most bucks will come in during the first ten minutes, but some just take their good old time.

I've used just about every rattling device on the market to rattle in deer. I'm convinced that when the time is right and the buck is in the mood, what you rattle with makes little or no difference, that buck is coming. I've had a number of bucks come to the sound of the bell on my dog's collar and I know guys who have rattled in bucks by clattering a couple of aluminum arrows together or shaking the chain on their tree stand.

With that said, I will say that I prefer a real set of antlers over all others. I've used my rattling antlers a long time. I've got faith in them. They feel good in my hands, like my favorite bow or hunting knife. And nothing sounds as much like the real thing as the real thing does,

although again, I don't think that authenticity counts for much with the deer.

I've always got something to rattle with. During peak rattling periods, I usually carry my rattling horns, but at other times of the year, you won't find me without a rattling bag or other rattling device. Many times, I have rattled in deer when I

Rattling works during the firearms season wherever the firearms season overlaps with the rut.

had no intention of doing any rattling that day. I could not have done that if I had not been in the habit of carrying some type of rattling device with me on every trip to the woods.

Whenever I am rattling from a tree stand using real antlers, I always tie my rattling antlers to my pull-up rope after I have retrieved my gun or bow. I got into

This 8.2-year-old buck is the oldest buck I have ever taken. Even though he was going downhill when I killed him, he was still responding to the horns.

this habit after an incident that occurred way back in November 1977. That's a long time ago, I know, but I remember that morning with excruciating clarity. I was hunting a woods in southern Minnesota and was busy banging those horns together when all of a sudden a monster whitetail burst out of a briar patch just to my right, not 15 steps away.

I guess I had been making so much noise with the antlers that I had not heard him coming. There was no question that this buck was looking for a fight. His ears were pinned back like a mad tomcat's and his hair was standing erect, which made him appear even larger than his already formidable size. I will not even venture a guess as to what his antlers would score. I know that I had never and have never since had an opportunity at a nontypical of such proportions. Of course, as soon as the buck burst from the briars, he realized that the sound was not coming from ground level, so he looked up to see what the two bucks he heard were doing fighting 20 feet up an oak tree. I panicked, pitched the rattling antlers into midair and frantically lunged for my recurve that was hanging from a branch stub a few feet away. When those horns hit the ground a few yards in front of the buck, you would think he would have turned inside out getting out of there, but evidently, the old boy was so pumped up with testosterone that he was not thinking too clearly. When I got my hands on my bow and glanced down again, the monster buck was pawing the ground like an old bull. He was itching for a fight, but he was not real sure what to fight. A cool customer would have drawn down on him and killed him. I was not cool. I tried to draw, but only managed to shake the arrow right off of the shelf. The arrow clattered down through the branches and hit the ground a few yards from where the buck was pawing dirt. I figured he would run off for sure, but he did not. I fumbled around, managed to pull another arrow from my quiver, got it on the string, jerked it back and sent that arrow sailing off in the general vicinity of the buck. The arrow must have whizzed by close enough to get the buck's attention,

because he quit pawing, took a long look around and simply walked away. I was shaking so badly that I was sure I was going to pitch right out of the tree. A few minutes later, I climbed down to retrieve my rattling antlers and my arrow. I only had three arrows and I wanted to make sure I had my full complement in the tree with me. I found the arrow lodged in a deadfall and after prying it loose, I picked up my rattling antlers and started back for the tree. Maybe I inadvertently let those antlers clack together, or maybe it was just my footsteps in the dry leaves that again attracted the huge buck. I heard a commotion in that briar patch, turned to look and there we stood, face to face. My bow was still hanging on that branch stub in the tree.

That's why I secure my rattling antlers to my pull-up rope. Now if a buck catches me with the horns in my hands, I just pitch them to the ground and grab my gun or bow. Twice, the habit has resulted in a nice buck on the ground. Many more times I have elected not to shoot, or the buck has not presented a shot. Either way, at least I do not have to climb down and retrieve my rattling antlers.

Another neat thing about this trick is that if the buck hangs up out of range or behind cover, just jiggle the rope and the antlers will clatter together at the base of your tree. Not only will this encourage the buck to come on in, but now his focus is on the ground and not up in the air.

Chapter Twelve

DECOYING

It was the end of the first week of November. Things were really cranking up in the whitetail world. The bucks were making a real nuisance of themselves pestering the does. Any day now, I knew that the first wave of does would come into estrous. This is an exciting time if you are a deer hunter. For me, it was even more exciting than usual that evening, because the day before I had seen a huge whitetail buck chasing does in the same alfalfa field over which I was now hunting. I was hoping that he would show up again. Everything was in my favor for that to happen. There were seventeen other deer in the field by late that afternoon. Mostly does, fawns and a couple of immature hoping-to-get-lucky bucks acting goofy. When all seventeen deer suddenly stopped what they were doing and stared toward a dip in the field, I knew that they had their eye on something special. He was special alright. I've seen only three bucks of his caliber. He looked

Hunting over a decoy adds a lot of enjoyment to the hunt. And it's a great way to position bucks for a good shot as well.

Use an orange mesh bag to transport the decoy if hunting an area where other hunters are present.

duced my best rendition of an estrous doe in desperate need of attention. It must have been pretty good, because the buck stopped in mid-stride, looked in my direction, spotted my decoy and headed my way. That's when my right leg began to jump.

While I fought for control of my nerves, I told myself two things over and over and over again: "Pick a spot and don't look at those horns." Once, many years ago, when I first began bowhunting, a heavy-horned Minnesota nontypical had ambled down the fence line I was hunting and passed within spitting distance of the wind-twisted box elder tree where I stood balancing precariously on a mostly horizontal branch about ten feet off the ground. When I drew back the old recurve and released, my cedar arrow went right where I was looking, clattering around in that mass of bone atop the buck's head before falling harmlessly to the leaves. I was not about to repeat that mistake.

Mr. Big never broke stride as he closed the distance. He was at 20 yards walking straight in and everything (except that jumping right leg) looked perfect. But then I heard the sound of deer running hard in the timber to my right and a sec-

like a sumo wrestler crashing a midget convention when he stepped into that field.

The buck was about 200 yards away from where I perched in an elevated tree stand at the far corner of the field. I grunted to get his attention, but if he heard the grunts, he ignored them. I didn't dare risk rattling, there were too many other deer between me and the big boy and I was afraid one of them would spot the movement and sound the alarm. So I depressed the reed on my call and pro-

ond later a doe burst out of the woods and blew into the alfalfa field with a scrubby little buck hot on her tail. As they dashed past the big buck, the bruiser simply turned around and walked directly away from me. I drew and grunted with my voice. The buck stopped and turned his head, but he would not turn his body to give me the shot I needed. A few more steps and I stopped him once more, but again he did not present me with the shot. The little buck and the doe had also skidded to a halt when I had grunted the first time. When the big boy fixed his gaze on that little buck, the youngster slunk off like a whipped dog. The big buck then turned his attention to the doe. When he turned to approach the doe, he was broadside at what I estimated to be 40 yards, but in the fading light I misjudged the range and my yellow and white fletching slipped just under his massive chest. The buck was so focused on the doe, that he paid no heed to the arrow diving harmlessly into the alfalfa beyond him. When he was gone, I was shaking so badly, I had to sit down or risk falling right off of my stand.

Okay, so I didn't connect on the big buck, but that episode, which took place in the rugged hill country of southwest

An easy way to use two decoys is to stuff a folding decoy inside the cavity of a full-bodied decoy.

Wisconsin, is a perfect example of why I love hunting over a deer decoy. Action. Hunting over a decoy is fun, not to mention the fact that a decoy will afford you shots at deer that otherwise would never present you with the opportunity.

Decoying deer is easy too. And no matter where you hunt, if there are whitetail around, they can be enticed to pay a decoy a visit. It does not matter if you hunt a 40-acre woodlot in New Jersey, a suburb of Chicago, the big timber of upstate New York, the cornfields of the Midwest, the prairies of Kansas or the piney woods of the Southeast, decoying during the rut will work.

When it comes to decoying deer during the rut, placement and positioning of the decoy are vital to success. So are factors like visibility, timing, odor control and finally, choosing the right decoy for your style of hunting.

Let's start with how to position your decoy, because this is one of the biggest mistakes I see hunters make when using a decoy.

In all cases, the wind should be blowing from the decoy to your stand or at the very worst a cross wind. Attempting to hunt over a decoy with the breeze blowing from you to the decoy, no matter how careful you are about odor control, is just asking for trouble.

My decoy is never more than 20 yards from my stand and often much closer. I do this so that if a buck hangs up beyond the decoy, which a few are going to do, chances are good that the deer will still be within my range.

When using a buck decoy, face the decoy toward the stand. I know that you

Hunters have more choices when it comes to deer decoys today, than they have ever had.

have heard and read that you should never face a decoy toward the stand. The reason always cited for this erroneous advice is that when a deer sees another deer staring in one direction it will look in that direction also and may spot you. The only thing I can say about this information is that it was probably passed along by someone who had very limited experience with decoying deer. Every hunter I know who is serious about decoying faces a buck decoy toward the stand. The reason for this is that when a buck approaches a buck decoy, it will nearly always circle around the decoy and come in head to head or at least head to shoulder. If the decoy is facing your position, the buck will provide you with a perfect broadside or quartering shot.

With a doe decoy, the opposite is true. Face the doe decoy either facing directly away or quartering away. A buck will nearly always approach a doe decoy from the rear, because that is the end of the doe he is most interested in.

The farther away a buck can spot your decoy, the better the odds that he will commit to your decoy. Field edges are ideal locations for a decoy. So are sloughs, clear-cuts, cut-lines and fence lines. A couple of the parcels of timber I hunt each fall are pastured all summer, so undergrowth is scant. A decoy will work in relatively open stands of mature timber, or woods that have been pastured, but in heavy cover, where a deer is going

to be right on top of the decoy before it can see the decoy, a decoy will cost you opportunities. I've seen bucks turn tail and run like the wind when suddenly encountering a decoy at close range.

Because whitetail deer are social creatures, a deer might investigate a decoy at anytime during the season. However, the most consistent action over a decoy will occur during the rut. The very best period in my experience is the ten-day to two-week long stretch just prior to the first wave of does coming into estrous. It is during this time that bucks will go out of their way to investigate the sound of grunt calls and rattling that I commonly use to draw a bucks attention to the decoy. Running a distant second is the actual breeding phase of the rut. You can still decoy plenty of immature bucks during this period, but be warned that most of the big boys are with the ladies and are not likely to give up on the real thing for an encounter with a fake.

A decoy that smells like a human won't cut it. Even a trace of human odor on the decoy will spook a buck. To prevent contaminating my decoys with human odor, I wear rubber or heavy, clean canvas gloves when handling the decoy. Once the decoy is in position, I spray down the entire decoy with a liquid odor neutralizer.

You do not need to add deer scent to a decoy to make it effective, but the addition of scent will hold deer around your decoy a little longer. This gives you more

Antler size on buck decoys is a personal preference. I like them big enough so that they are visible at a good distance, but not so big that they will scare off all but the biggest bucks.

scent wick and apply the scent to the wick. I usually use a doe-in-estrous urine when using a doe decoy and a buck urine or tarsal gland scent when using a buck decoy. Some hunters like to rub a slice of apple or the meat of an acorn on the nose of their decoy for a little added attraction.

Which decoy is right for you depends upon a number of factors. Cost for instance. You can purchase a decoy for under $100 or plunk down nearly a grand. Portability is another consideration. If you are going to be hiking long distances to reach the places where you can use your decoy, you don't want a 3-D decoy. Silhouettes are the way to go if this is your circumstance. No, silhouettes are not as effective as full-bodied decoys, but they are a whole lot more effective than you might think. I use them a lot when I hike into a distant stand. But if I can drive near to or right up to my stand

time to make a good shot. I don't like to use scent directly on the decoy. Instead, I take a stick and jam it in the ground beneath the decoy. On the stick I hang an absorbent

The Montana Decoy, a folding, polyester photographic image, is the lightest and most portable of all of the decoys. Supported by a spring steel band, the decoy collapses into a 2-pound, 2 x 16-inch packet.

with an ATV or my pickup, I'll go with a full-body. If hunting the evening, I'll try to drive in and drop off my decoys at midday. If hunting the morning, I'll take them in the day before and stash the decoys in a deadfall or brush pile.

In the right situation, hunting over a decoy during the rut is very deadly. But most of all, hunting over a decoy is a lot of fun. I won't guarantee that you will shoot the biggest buck of your life if you use a decoy, but I will guarantee that you will have more fun hunting and hey, isn't that the main reason we hunt?

Chapter Thirteen

CALLING
the RUT

The buck cruising along the hillside 75 yards below my stand was on a mission. His assignment? To find himself a willing doe. Like most bucks during the rut, this one was covering some ground in an attempt to do just that. Head down, nose to the ground, he moved at a steady, ground eating fast walk. I needed him closer. I grabbed my grunt tube and hit him with a series of grunts, but the buck was making so much racket shuffling through the frost-coated carpet of fallen leaves,

Mixing in some grunts with a rattling sequence is a good way to add realism to your rattling.

Calling is a way to put some action into the hunt. That is important when introducing youngsters, who tend to get bored easily anyway, to the hunt.

that he never heard me. I blew the call louder. What came out the other end of that grunt tube did not sound anything like any deer I have ever heard, but by golly, that buck heard it. He stopped in his tracks. As soon as he turned his head to look away from my direction, I gave a couple of quick grunts. That was all the stocky eight-pointer needed. He turned and hustled up the hill. I tucked the call back in my jacket, grabbed my bow off of the hook and when the buck posed at 15 yards, I sent a broadhead slipping through his lungs.

No, calling a deer is not always that easy, but it is often enough that every serious whitetail hunter should be carrying a grunt tube with him. A buck during the rut that does not have a doe is a real sucker for calling.

It seems sometimes like deer calls have been commonplace forever, but actually, even though there have been deer calls around since the '60s, the idea that you could actually call deer did not become popular until the late '80s and early '90s. Of course today, it is rare to find a deer hunter who does not own at least one deer call. Game call manufacturers have done a good job of marketing. But even though most hunters today know that deer can and do communicate, I find that the majority of hunters I come in contact with are reluctant to use that call draped around their neck. They are afraid, I think, that they will call at the wrong time or blow a bad note and scare deer away. In my experience that is not likely. Calling deer is easy. Compared to calling elk, predators, crows, ducks or geese, it is child's play. Nobody should ever be afraid to try to call deer.

During the past two decades there have been numerous scientific studies done on whitetail deer vocalizations. The one I refer to most often was conducted in 1988 at the University of Georgia by Karl Miller, Larry Marchinton and Tom Atkinson. These researchers identified 90 different sounds made by whitetail deer. They then categorized these sounds and came up with twelve different groups of vocalizations used by deer. Don't worry, you don't have to learn all 90 or even all twelve groups to call deer effectively, but you might be interested to know what they are. The twelve groups are the mew, bleat, nursing whine, maternal grunt, contact grunt, tending grunt, low grunt, bawl, grunt-snort-wheeze, Flehmen sniff, grunt snort and probably the one that every deer hunter in North America has heard, the snort. I take it one step further and break these twelve down into just three basic vocalizations, the grunt, the bleat and the snort. Let's take a look at each of them.

THE GRUNT
The grunt is the vocalization that most deer hunters associate with whitetail deer and the vocalization they most often mimic on their calls. Many hunters think that only bucks grunt, but that's not true. Does make a maternal grunt, but it is a very low volume grunt and you must be very close to the deer and be blessed with excellent hearing to hear it. The maternal grunt is not a grunt you would try to make to bring a deer closer to you. The three grunts you should rely upon are the contact grunt, trailing grunt and tending grunt. Learn these three and you will call bucks.

CONTACT GRUNT
The contact grunt is used by bucks at all times of the year. I have found it to be most effective early in the season and during post-rut. This is not an aggressive grunt, nor is it in any way associated with the rut. The contact grunt is just a buck's way of asking if there are any other deer within hearing. Often, I have watched

One of the things I really like about calling is that it works at anytime of the season.

bucks walking through the woods just suddenly stop and give a contact grunt. When a buck hears another buck make a contact grunt, that buck will often walk over to check the other buck out. That is what makes the contact grunt so effective. Most of the bucks I've had respond to a contact grunt have arrived in a relaxed state of mind, or at least relaxed for a whitetail. This is because a buck responding to a contact grunt is not expecting trouble. Because the contact grunt is a soft, low-volume grunt, I have found it to be most effective on bucks that are in sight, but out of range.

One tip I should pass along to you regarding the contact grunt is that even though it is a short, soft, quiet grunt, depending upon conditions, you may need to grunt much louder than an actual contact grunt to get the buck's attention. I try to wait until a buck is standing still before I grunt at him, but sometimes a buck is just shuffling along and does not stop. If that buck is walking in dry leaves, or even dry grass, it is very difficult for him to hear a soft contact grunt. When you are faced with this predicament, do not be afraid to really lay into that grunt call. Get that buck's attention any way you can. Once you have his attention, then you can try to entice him with a contact grunt at normal volume.

THE TRAILING GRUNT

In the Georgia study, which I referred to earlier, the trailing grunt was not identified. I suspect that the researchers lumped the trailing and tending grunts together and if you wish to do that as well, I won't be offended. However, even though I am not a wildlife biologist or trained researcher, in my experience there is a definite difference between the vocalizations a buck makes while he is trailing a doe and the grunts the buck makes when actually tending a doe.

Like the contact grunt, the trailing grunt is short in duration, but is much louder than the contact grunt and is usually repetitious. I can sense the buck's urgency and his excitement in the trailing grunt, while there is none of either in the contact grunt.

Just as no two of us talk alike, no two bucks make the same trailing grunt. Some bucks grunt with each step, while others might grunt only every ten steps and still others maybe only once or twice in the length of a football field. I've seen a few bucks hot on the trail of a hot doe that did not grunt at all while they were within my hearing range. The fact that not all bucks sound the same or have the same cadence or rhythm to their grunts is good news for us hunters, because what that means is that there is really no wrong way to mimic the trailing grunt. When I'm calling blind, which means that there is not a buck in sight, I tend to go with a long series of grunts, often 20 or more. If a buck is in sight, I call only until I have the buck's attention. You never want to call while a buck is looking in your direction. A white-tail deer might not be quite as sharp at pin-pointing the precise source of a call as some critters, namely the coyote and wild turkeys, but he won't miss it by much, so calling when a deer is looking your way is just asking for trouble.

One tip I can give you on using the trailing grunt is this: When you are call-ing blind, start with the tube of the grunt call pointed over the back of your right shoulder and as you call, slowly move the call around in front of you until you finish with it pointed over your left shoulder. This helps to give the impression of a deer on the move and since I have never seen a buck stand in one place and deliver a repetitious trail-ing grunt, this little trick cannot help but add realism to your calling.

THE TENDING GRUNT

When a buck is actually tending a doe, he has two things on his mind. One is trying to keep that doe confined to a small area. The second is protecting his prize from rival bucks. I've heard bucks make some mighty strange sounds while accomplishing this mission. One time, I had a monster buck tending a doe up in the coulee country of Wisconsin's justifi-ably famous Buffalo County that sound-ed like an old three-horsepower outboard motor I used on my duckboat many years ago. That buck could utter that low, guttural growl nonstop for minutes at a time. I had both the buck and the doe within sight for about a half-hour and once had the buck as close as 40 yards but there was too much brush to risk a shot.

Like the trailing grunt, feel free to experiment when making tending grunts. I doubt that I ever play the same tune twice when cutting loose with a string of tending grunts. One thing I do try to do is to really draw out the grunts. The con-tact grunt is a single, abrupt grunt. The trailing grunt is a series of abrupt grunts. But the tending grunt should feature a combination of short grunts and long, drawn-out grunts.

I've had some of my best action while using the tending grunt just before the does come into estrous and again late in the rut after most of the does have been bred. This makes sense. Right before the first does come into estrous, a whitetail buck is a real basket case. If he hears what he thinks is another buck tending a doe, he can't help himself, he has got to check it out. On the other end of the rut, I've found that while the majority of younger bucks may have lost the urge, the big boys have not. Even after most of the does have been bred, the big breeder bucks are still on the prowl, looking for

The canister-type call is excellent for delivering authentic sounding doe bleats. Just turn it over and when you bring it back right side up, it will bleat.

one more opportunity to help procreate the species. When one of these bucks hears a tending grunt, he knows exactly what it means.

THE DOE BLEAT

I was guilty of not using a doe bleat for many years and I know now that was a mistake on my part. Over the past few seasons, I've called in a number of bucks by using the doe bleat by itself, but mainly I use a doe bleat in combination with a trailing or tending grunt. My success rate has shown a dramatic improvement since I incorporated the doe bleat into my little symphony in the woods.

There are two ways you can mix a few doe bleats in with your tending or trailing grunts. One way is to use a variable tone grunt call. With the True-Talker grunt call I have been using the past few seasons, it is as simple as applying finger pressure to slightly different locations on the enclosed reed. Other variable tone grunt calls use buttons or plungers. The advantage to a variable tone grunt call is that you do not have to switch calls when mixing doe bleats in with your grunts.

Another slick way of producing the doe bleat is to use a "call-in-a-can." Primos, for instance, has three different sizes of the can: the smallest designed for close-range calling, the original can intended for mid-range calling and the "Great Big

Variable tone grunt calls have eliminated the need for carrying multiple calls around your neck.

Can," which really is not all that big but is slightly louder than the other two. With any of the three, all you have to do is hold the can in your hand, tip it over and upright it again and the can emits a very authentic sounding doe bleat. With a grunt call in one hand and a can in the other, it is very easy to mix doe bleats in with your tending and trailing grunts.

If, like me, you have been using a grunt call for a number of years but have not tried doe bleats, do yourself a favor this season and work a few doe bleats into your calling.

I think that like me, you will probably be pleasantly surprised with the results.

THE SNORT

The grunt-snort-wheeze and grunt snort are both very aggressive vocalizations. They are invariably made by one buck as he warns another buck to keep his distance. You will often hear one or more often both bucks make one of these vocalizations and most generally the grunt-snort-wheeze right before they lower their heads and come together in battle. I know that calls that mimic the grunt-snort-wheeze have been so-so popular for a number of years and I suppose I should, just in the name of research, use one in my own hunting, but I just can't bring myself to do it. I keep asking myself, "Why would I want to imitate a sound that is intended not to attract, but to repel?" A grunt-snort-wheeze is a warning. Stay away from me or else is the clear message.

Granted, if the buck that hears the grunt-snort-wheeze is the biggest, baddest buck in the neighborhood, he might just be inclined to accept the invitation. But what if the buck hearing the grunt-snort-wheeze is instead a mighty fine ten-pointer that just so happens to have had his butt kicked lately. You think that buck is going to respond to a grunt-snort-wheeze? Not hardly.

Let me close this chapter on calling during the rut with this little tidbit of personal insight. Over the years, it has been my great pleasure to get to know some mighty fine deer hunters. Some of these hunters are famous in deer hunting circles, many are not. All of them have different ideas when it comes to deer hunting. All employ different tactics. But

Deer calls are very easy to use. With just a minimum of preseason practice, you will be ready to call deer.

all of them, without exception, rely heavily on calling to put good bucks in front of them. If you are not calling during the rut, you are missing out on some good action.

Chapter Fourteen

DEER SCENTS
and the RUT

Sometime back in the early 1960s, when I was just a kid getting started in deer hunting, I walked into the local fur buyer's shop one afternoon with an armload of muskrat pelts. The fur buyer, like fur buyers everywhere, inspected every pelt, running his hand up inside the cased pelt, blowing on the long guard hairs, tracing every slip of my skinning knife with his arthritic fingers. By the time he was finished, I figured I was darn lucky to get the 75 cents per pelt he offered. When I stepped to the counter to get my money, there was a cardboard box sitting on the counter with a crude, hand-lettered sign, which simply read "Buck Lure $1.00." I sprung for one of the small, glass vials and I've been using deer scents ever since. I know that I have dipped, dripped, dribbled, sprayed or spilled a 55-gallon drum of the stuff over the years.

Clockwise: To make a mock scrape, use a stout stick or a garden trowel to clear away all of the grass and debris from beneath an overhanging branch. Dig a hole a couple of inches deep and bury a Buc-Rut scent wafer in the hole. Pour about a cup of Magic Scrape into the scrape you have made. This is a scent-impregnated, waterproof soil that holds scent for a long time and seems to really attract bucks to the scrape. Make a depression in the mound of Magic Scrape.

I've had as much experience with deer scents as any hunter I know and a lot more than most, and I will be the first to tell you that deer scents do not work all of the time. In fact, they do not work half of the time. But they do their job often enough that they are darn sure worth using.

Deer scents will work at anytime of the season, but they are most effective during the rut. When the bucks are in a breeding mood, they are very interested in scents. After all, it is very often their sense of smell that leads them to an estrous doe. With the correct use of deer scents, you can make that sensitive sense of smell work for you, instead of against you.

There are many different ways to use deer scents. The ones that have been most effective for me when hunting during the rut have been laying down a scent trail, doctoring scrapes, making mock scrapes, positioning scent wicks around my stand site and what I call airborne scents. Let's take a look at each of these scent tactics.

SCENT TRAILS

It was during that murky time between full night and the dawn when the first buck came slipping over the ridge. His nose was to the ground and he traveled with a singleness of purpose, which is common of whitetail bucks during the rut. His mission? Find the doe that had left the trail of tantalizing scent. This buck was in for a disappointment. There was no hot doe waiting at the end of this trail. Only me

sitting in a tree stand, the bow resting across my knees with an arrow nocked. I studied the buck through binoculars as he approached. At 70 yards, the buck finally stopped and lifted his head for a look around, giving me my first good look at his rack. An eight-point spreading just beyond his ears, I quickly judged the buck to be a fine two-and-one-half-year-old buck. A good buck, but not the caliber of buck I was looking for on this hunt. The buck dropped his head and never picked it up again until the trail he was following suddenly came to an abrupt dead end under the branches of a maple sapling 20 yards in front of my perch. When the buck hit the end of the trail, he stopped, lifted his head, looked around and then got a whiff of the drag rag I had hung from the branches of the maple. For a minute or two, the buck rubbed his face and antlers against the drag rag, occasionally stopping to lick and sniff the scent-laden strip of cloth. Then, with a quick flick of his tail, the usual signal that a whitetail deer has lost interest in something, the buck walked off.

My hunter's log shows that I sat in that stand the rest of the day and saw a total of six bucks, five of which followed the scent trail I had laid down in the dark that morning on my way to my stand. Since the scent trail I had laid down to that particular stand cut through a wide swath of timber on the opposite side of the ridge from where my stand was located, there is an excellent chance that had it not been for the scent trail, I would have seen only one buck that day, the lone buck that I saw on my side of the ridge. That is the beauty of a scent trail; it allows you to see deer that you otherwise would never have laid eyes on.

I've been bringing bucks past my stand for 30 years using doe-in-estrous urine. I've tried other scents, including buck, doe and fawn urine, tarsal gland scent and a scent that incorporates interdigital gland and there are times when I incorporate an interdigital gland scent with doe-in-estrous urine, but over the years, nothing has been as effective as a doe-in-estrous urine. Doe-in-estrous scents are most effective around the time of the rut, but I do not hesitate to use a doe-in-estrous scent trail at anytime during the season. From the time a buck sheds his velvet until he casts his antlers, he is capable of breeding. My theory is that a buck is not smart enough to know that he should not be smelling a doe in heat in mid-September or late December. If she is ready, he is ready, no matter what the date on the calendar. And since I have only witnessed a buck spook from a doe-in-estrous scent on one occasion and that was a clear case of me

Fill the depression with your favorite scent.

overdoing a good thing, I see no reason not to use a doe-in-estrous scent trail regardless of the date. However, I must warn you of the only drawback to using a doe-in-estrous scent I am aware of. On several occasions, I have had does become snakey when encountering a doe-in-estrous scent. If there happens to be a buck with the doe and the doe gets nervous and leaves, you can bet the buck is going with her. This has not happened often, but it has occurred often enough that I felt it only fair to warn you of the possibility.

Over the years I have used scent from most of the scent manufacturers. It appears to me that doe-in-estrous urine is doe-in-estrous urine and the label on the bottle is unimportant. I've also used those "special" doe-in-estrous urines that are guaranteed to be fresh. While I have enjoyed some excellent results with these "special delivery" estrous lures the last couple of seasons, I cannot say unequivocally that they are any better than the estrous lures that have been on the shelf for a month or two. My advice is to try a few different brands until you find one that works for you and then stick with it. Even though I believe there is little, if any, difference between various brands of doe-in-estrous urine, using one that has produced in the past will give you a big boost in the confidence department and we all know how important confidence is in deer hunting.

There are two important points to keep in mind when laying down a scent trail. One, the amount of scent you leave on the ground should remain fairly constant or increase as you near the stand site. And second, there should not be any gaps of more than a couple of feet in the scent trail. I've learned both of these lessons the hard way.

For many years I used a "drag-rag" to lay down scent trails. My drag rag was a strip of clean cotton cloth about two inches wide by six to ten inches long, usually a worn-out diaper, since we were in the baby years around our house back then. I would tie the strip of cloth to a five-foot-long length of twine. When I got to where I wanted to begin laying down a scent trail, I would apply a few drops of urine to the rag, let the rag drag behind me as I walked 50 yards or so and then apply a couple more drops to the rag. What I didn't know was that by being so stingy with the scent, I was not leaving much of a scent trail to begin with and what scent I did leave was decreasing in potency as I neared my stand. Then one afternoon I had been in my stand for only a half-hour when I spotted a nice buck cutting across the same harvested cornfield I had crossed on my hike into my stand. When the buck crossed my scent trail, he stuck his nose to the ground and came stiff-legging it in my direction. I started to shake, but my excitement was premature. Suddenly the buck stopped, turned around in his tracks and followed the scent trail in the wrong direction, finally disappearing into the woods on the opposite end of the harvested cornfield. I wanted to stand up and holler, "No, no, you dummy, you're supposed to come this way!" But, of course, the real dummy was sitting in the tree. The buck was just doing what any animal following a scent will do and that is following the trail in the

Spray the overhanging branch with scent.

direction in which the scent grows stronger. Today, there are dozens of scent applicators available that do a good job of laying down a consistent and unbroken scent trail and I prefer these over the old drag rag. However, if you want to save a couple of bucks and use a drag rag, just be sure to use plenty of scent on the rag to start with and freshen the scent often as you hike into the stand.

My favorite system for laying down a scent trail is to use fresh tarsal glands. These glands, taken from bucks during the rut, seem to be most effective, although I have had results with tarsal glands that were taken from bucks prior to the rut. Fresh tarsal glands are not hard to come by. I acquire them from road kill bucks, bucks taken by buddies or bucks I kill myself. Wearing rubber gloves, I use a sharp knife and skin the tarsal gland from the inside of each hind leg and cut a slit through the hide of each tarsal gland. Each tarsal is dropped into a separate plastic bag. I leave one tarsal "plain" and add about a half ounce of doe-in-heat urine to the bag with the other tarsal. I store the tarsals in my refrigerator between hunts. When I get

Either use a Buc-Rut scent wafer or a scent wick on the overhanging branch.

to where I want to begin laying down the scent trail, I tie both tarsals to a short rope and let them drag behind me as I hike into my stand. A tarsal gland can easily absorb one-half ounce of scent and does a good job of laying down a consistent scent trail. I have found it unnecessary to add more scent at intervals as I lay down the trail. However, I do freshen up the tarsal with more scent before each hunt. I have tried to freeze the tarsal glands and keep them from one season to the next, and I have tried the freeze-dried tarsals you can buy, but I have not had near the success with these "reconstituted" tarsals as I have enjoyed with fresh tarsal glands.

Scent trails greatly increase your odds of seeing bucks anytime you are hunting in terrain or habitat that makes it possible for a buck to slip past you unseen. I've hunted whitetail deer in over 20 states and provinces and on only a handful of occasions have I sat in stands where I had the luxury of being able to see well enough and far enough in all directions that I felt certain a buck could not sneak past without my spotting him. These stands are normally thin bands of connecting timber or similarly tight funnel situations. Ninety percent of the time when I am bowhunting and often when hunting with a gun, I will have a scent trail leading to my stand from at least one direction.

Most of the advice you hear concerning scent trails suggests laying down a trail for only 100 or 200 yards. Me, I'm a believer in long-range scent trails. I've seen bucks follow a scent trail for 500 yards and I once backtracked a buck I killed on a scent trail after a fresh overnight snow and found that the buck had cut my scent trail just over 1,000 of my steps away from my stand. Whitetail deer are curious critters and even when the rut is not a major factor, bucks will follow a scent trail for a long way just out of curiosity. After all, unlike you and I who lead busy lives, that buck probably does not have anything better to do.

There is nothing scientific about laying down a scent trail. You have to walk into your stand anyway, so why not pull a drag rag behind you. You never know, like me, the biggest buck of your life may one day come sniffing his way along the scent trail you laid down.

SCENTING SCRAPES

In the gathering gloom of a late November dusk, the big buck heard the sound of clashing antlers reverberating through the

If you use a scent wick, saturate the wick until it will not hold anymore scent.

river bottoms. Although the distinctive clatter of bone-on-bone was over 300 yards away, the buck instantly pinpointed the precise source of the sound, spun on big, blunt-toed hooves and bee-lined toward the sound. I heard his hooves pounding the hard, sun-baked Kansas clay, let the rattling bag drop to my side on its lanyard and plucked the Mathews off of the bow hook. The buck jumped a sagging, barbed wire fence 30 yards away and straight downwind of where I perched 20 feet up a gnarly, wind-tortured cottonwood. When he skidded to a sudden halt behind a thick stand of scrub willow, I figured that, despite all of my precautions to control my human odor, the old buck had picked up just a whiff of human scent and was now letting his brain determine whether the dreaded scent was near enough or fresh enough to be of concern. It seemed like forever, but it was probably only 30 seconds before the buck's brain gave him the "no sweat" answer. The buck curled around the point of the willow patch and went directly to a scrape that I had "tuned up" hours earlier. The buck's antlers were hooking the overhanging willow branch when my broadhead sliced silently through both of his lungs.

That buck happens to be the most recent buck I've taken over a tuned-up scrape, but he darn sure was not the first and he won't be the last. I'm a big fan of tuning up scrapes, but despite the success I've enjoyed hunting over them, I won't sit here and try to convince you that all you have to do to see more bucks and bigger bucks is to pour some pee in a scrape and get ready for a buck parade. It does not work that way. I've carefully scented a lot of scrapes and then hunted over them without ever seeing a buck. So why bother? Because over the past 20 years I have had more bucks visit scrapes that I have tuned up with scent than have visited scrapes that have not been tuned up.

I believe that the biggest advantage you gain from adding scent to scrapes and overhanging branches is that the scent you add triggers a response from any buck visiting the scrape. Perhaps that response is one of aggression or dominance if a buck urine or tarsal gland scent is used. It may trigger sexual frustration if a doe-in-estrous urine is employed. Or maybe all scents simply trigger the natural curiosity of the whitetail. This I believe certainly helps explain why researchers have found bucks to sometimes be attracted to scrapes that have purposefully been tainted with human urine or other odors that we assume would spook, not attract, deer. The bottom line is that despite all of the research, you and I may never know what is really going through a buck's mind when he checks out a doctored scrape. And hey, who cares anyway? All I care about is making sure that if a buck is going to visit a scrape during shooting hours, that the scrape he selects is the one I'm sitting over. If you can make a buck remember that he smelled something good in a certain scrape, then you are on your way to accomplishing that goal.

When I first began messing around with deer scents and later when I began adding scents to scrapes, deciding what scent to use was easy. All we had was what we called "doe pee." Today, there are over 100 choices on the market. Scents based on deer urine are still the biggest sellers, but many have now added tarsal gland, interdigital gland and even forehead gland to the mix. Synthetics are big too. So are the so-called "solid scents," the pastes, gels, crystals and pellets. I have not used them all, but I have tested a lot of them and although I have had better results with some than others, I would not conclude that my in-the-field tests really prove anything. If a buck happens to visit a scrape I've tuned up with product A on Monday but I don't see a buck while hunting over a scrape juiced up with product B on Tuesday, does it mean that product A is more attractive to bucks than product B? I

Everything you need for making mock scrapes.

don't think so. Instead, I pick my "favorites" using a different criteria. How long does a buck hang around when he visits one of my tuned-up scrapes? If a buck spends a lot of time sniffing and licking at the scrape and overhanging branch, then I figure whatever scent I used has really got his attention. I've had bucks spend over ten minutes at scrapes I've scented. One Illinois buck came back to visit a scrape I was sitting over six times in one day. I figured that little seven-pointer had a death wish, but I did not grant his wish. But you can bet that the scent I was using in that scrape is on my all-time-favorites list.

More important than what brand of scent you leave behind at the scrape is the brand of scent you do not leave behind. I'm talking about human odor of course. When I tune up a scrape, I wear a Scent-Lok suit, rubber boots (often hip boots) and rubber gloves. A mature buck lives by his nose and if his nose tells him that a human has been at his scrape, then I don't care what brand of

When I hike to my stand, I nearly always lay down a scent trail. Like most things in deer hunting, a scent trails does not always work, but it works often enough to be worth the effort.

scent you use, odds are good that buck will never visit that scrape again.

To tune up a scrape, I begin by using a stick or a garden trowel to work up the soil in the scrape. Usually, I work in some gel or paste lure at the same time. If it is a scrape that I know I might not be able to hunt for several days, I bury an H.S Buc-Rut scent wafer an inch under the soil or I take a small jar or 35mm film canister, add scent, poke some holes in the lid and bury it an inch or so under the surface.

Next, I pour a large handful of Magic Scrape into the center of the scrape. Magic Scrape is a specially blended, waterproof soil that bucks find very attractive by itself, but I spice it up a little by making a depression in the mound of Magic Scrape and adding a half-ounce of liquid scent. That's it for the scrape, now onto the really important stuff, the overhanging branch.

Every scrape worth hunting over has an overhanging branch and it is here that the real scent communication between deer takes place. Many times I have watched deer come into a scrape and never even bother to sniff the scrape itself, but spend minutes licking, chewing, rubbing and hooking the overhanging branch with their antlers. A buck leaves scent behind from his tarsal, saliva, forehead, nasal, and preorbital glands as well as his urine when he works an overhanging branch. Add a little of your favorite scent to the branch itself and then take a scent wick and secure it to the branch with wire or a plastic tie. Don't be cheap when it comes to applying scent to that scent wick, soak it until it won't hold anymore.

When I first began hunting over scrapes, I only had one criteria in choosing the scrape I hunted over—size. The bigger the better I figured. The problem with really big scrapes, or community scrapes as they are commonly called because these huge scrapes are nearly always the work of more than one buck, is that they are usually found on the edge of a major feeding location, which in most whitetail habitats means a field edge. Does gather here each night to feed. Bucks come to sniff the does. One buck walks over and paws out a scrape. As soon as he walks off another steps up to the plate and then the next and the next and the next. My friend Tom Indrebo, who runs Bluff Country Outfitters in western Wisconsin's famed Buffalo County, once placed a surveillance camera near such a scrape. In a single night, all 24 exposures fired. We checked the prints with an 8X lupe to make sure we did not count the same buck twice and came up with an astounding 21 different bucks visiting that scrape in one night. That's how you get a "community scrape." The problem with these big scrapes is that all of the action takes place at night. On rare occasions, when the testosterone is peaking in a mature buck's system, that buck may become so bold as to visit such a scrape during shooting hours, but I'm not willing to bet my season on those odds. Instead, I look for scrapes in the timber and preferably near but not in heavy cover. Such a location is one of my favorite places to pull an all-day sit, something I do quite often during the rut. Most deer get up out of their beds at midday to relieve themselves, stretch and browse a little. Big bucks are no exception. Many times, when the scraping phase of the rut is in full swing, a buck will check a nearby scrape or two during this midday activity period.

You will often read that the peak scrap-ing period of the rut occurs during the two weeks prior to the first does entering estrous and this information is accurate. During this two-week-long stretch, every buck in the timber gets into the scraping mode. The problem with this period is that if you are hunting an area with a decent buck population, there are too many scrapes. With so many scrapes, it is more difficult to elicit interest in your tuned-up scrape. Also, when scraping is at its peak, it is nearly impossible to concentrate your efforts on a mature buck. That is why my favorite time to tune up scrapes is before the peak of the scraping phase of the rut. Mature bucks begin scraping earlier, often as much as two weeks earlier than imma-ture bucks. Finding a big buck's scrapes takes some snooping, but I have found it to be worth the effort.

SCENT WICKS

Let me share with you several reasons why I am a big fan of hanging scent wicks around my stand each time I hunt.

It was very windy that October after-noon, so windy, that my friend Monte Nichols almost did not go hunting. But the thought of an especially large buck, which had been seen in the area a time or two, convinced him to go, wind or no wind. Before climbing into his tree stand, Monte hung several scent wicks doctored with a doe-in-estrous urine around his stand. An hour later when he looked back over his left shoulder there stood the monster buck with his nose up against one of those scent wicks. As you might expect, Monte was more than a little shook up by such a sight and the first time he tried to draw on the buck, his arrow rattled right off of his rest. The buck looked his way and Monte was sure that the next view he would have of the buck was the buck's fat ass disappearing into the timber. But the buck was so taken by the smell of that scent wick, that instead of bolting, the buck turned his attention back to the pleasant scent. Bad mistake on the buck's part.

Less than a month later and only a few miles as the crow flies from where Monte had taken his Boone & Crockett nontypical, another hunter climbed into his stand on another very windy day. Just as Monte had done, Richard hung a couple of doctored scent wicks near the trails intersecting below his stand. Smart move as it turned out. Like many hunters, Richard reads a paperback book on stand to help pass the long hours. Read a page, look and listen, read another page. Richard had been doing it for years, but on this day, because of the wind, the buck was right behind Richard and coming hard before Richard ever heard the buck. Richard knew that there was not going to be time to stash the paperback, grab his bow from the hanger and draw his bow before the buck, now right beneath his stand and moving fast, nose to the ground, like his kind do when feverishly searching for a hot doe, raced out of range. And then the buck

hit the scent stream from one of the scent wicks Richard had hung hours earlier. The buck skidded to a halt, followed his nose to the source of the tantalizing smell and probably never felt that broadhead slice neatly through his lungs.

And just to show that scent bombs are of benefit to gun hunters as well as bowhunters, allow me to share one of the many positive experiences I have had with scent bombs over the years. Several years ago while filming a show for the Realtree Outdoors television show and Monster Bucks video series, my stand on the last evening of my hunt overlooked a pair of long, narrow cut-lines. Before climbing into the stand that afternoon I had walked out to the cut-lines and deployed a couple of scent wicks on each. My hope was that any buck crossing the cut-line would get a whiff of the doe-in-estrous scent I had applied to the scent wicks and that the smell would cause the buck to investigate, which would give me more time to judge the buck and make the shot and would give the cameraman the time he needed to get on the buck and roll some tape before I pulled the trigger. Just before last light, I picked up my heavy rattling horns and for the umpteenth time that day sent the sound of two bucks duking it out rolling over the monotonous Canadian bush. This time an ancient buck, probably the oldest I have ever killed, came to investigate. On the TV show and in the video, what you see is the massive ten-point buck walking a

Doctoring scrapes is deadly when you have bucks actively working scrapes. They seem to want to know who that other buck is that has been at the scrape. That kind of curiosity can work in your favor.

weaving pattern in one of those cut-lines. The reason why the buck is weaving is that he was trying to pinpoint the source of the scent I had applied to those scent wicks.

Does that mean that every time you use scent wicks you can expect to see big bucks? Of course not, there are no magic pills in the world of hunting free-range whitetail deer. But I've proven to my satisfaction on dozens of occasions that using scent wicks can help hold a buck's attention while you draw your bow or move your rifle into position to make the shot. To me that is reason enough for using scent bombs. However, scent bombs also perform two other valuable functions. As the odor drifts downwind, any buck intercepting that odor is likely to follow his nose to the source. This means that scent bombs allow you to see deer that you likely otherwise would never lay eyes on. In addition, scent bombs can help to cover up human odor, although they will in no way make up for sloppy odor control.

Because I have deployed hundreds, probably thousands, of scent bombs over the past 30 years and have yet to have buck number one spook from a scent bomb, I rarely hunt from a stand without deploying a few scent wicks. The only negative response to scent wicks that I have ever witnessed have been from does, usually those old, long-necked, hump-nosed, ultra-fussy ones that seem to be nervous ninnies about anything and everything. On occasion, I have had a doe being trailed by a buck become nervous when she encountered the scent from one of my scent bombs and lead the buck away instead of toward my position. However, this occurrence is rare enough that I do not consider it a viable reason for not using scent bombs.

Before the first scent bombs, I simply applied my deer urine or lure to a shoulder-high branch or onto the trunk of a tree. After a season or two of that, I began using cotton balls and a few years later, like other hunters, I began stuffing cotton balls into empty 35mm film canisters. These were the original scent bombs and despite all of the various scent wicks and variations of the old scent bomb on the market today, if you are the cost-conscious type, you can make the old original scent bombs for pennies each (not counting the cost of the scent) and they still get the job done. If you decide to use the 35mm scent bomb, the most important thing to remember is to pluck the cotton up out of the canister to form a wick so that the breeze can get at the scent and carry it. During the 1980s, some hunters, including myself, began experimenting with tampons for use as scent bombs. They worked well and I suspect that the idea for scent wicks, which are the most popular of all the scent bombs on the market today, originated from that concept. These super absorbent wicks hold a lot of scent for a long time and because the entire surface is exposed to the air, that scent is easily transported on the slightest breeze or thermal.

There is no need to get fancy when it comes to deploying your scent wicks. For bow-hunting I use between four and eight wicks and arrange them in a circle around my stand. All of the scent wicks are within easy range of my stand. In fact, I often use the scent wicks as range markers. All scent wicks should be hung in spots that you can shoot to if a buck is standing with his nose to the scent wick. Hang the scent wicks three to five feet off the ground. Wear rubber gloves whenever you handle the scent wicks and don't be a penny-pincher with the scent, especially if you are going to be hunting more than just an hour or two. The more scent you apply, the longer it will take for the scent to evaporate and the better the odds that the scent wicks will still be working for you when you climb down from your stand.

I also frequently use a scent wick attached to the overhanging branch when doctoring a real scrape or making a mock scrape. The scent wick will hold scent much longer than if you simply apply the scent directly to the branch itself. Use a wire or sturdy plastic tie to attach the scent wick to the overhanging branch or bucks will tear it off with their mouths or antlers while working the branch.

When hunting with a gun, I often use scent wicks to encourage bucks to stop where I can get a good shot at them. Logging roads, senderos in South Texas, cut-lines in Canada, natural woodland openings—the possibilities are as varied as the terrain the whitetail inhabits.

And one last way in which you may want to employ a scent wick is to use it to hold

I always carry a spray bottle of scent with me and use it when deer get downwind of me. Sometimes it actually draws them to me, but even if it does not, it might prevent them from detecting me. Works really great when rattling.

your favorite cover scent. Simply apply the cover scent to the wicks and hang two or three of them around you in your stand.

MOCK SCRAPES MAKE THINGS HAPPEN

Before I get into why I use mock scrapes and how to prepare them, a short discussion on scraping behavior in whitetail deer is in order. A scrape is nothing more than a bare patch of earth about the size and shape of an oval laundry basket, although on occasion you will find much larger ones. A buck paws the ground to clear

away all of the leaves, sticks and grass and then urinates in the bare earth, often squeezing his hind legs together so that the urine dribbles over his tarsal glands, which are located on the inside of each hind leg. This adds a scent to the scrape that only another whitetail could find appealing.

Hanging over the scrape itself will be an overhanging branch, usually a live branch, somewhere between four and five and one-half feet off the ground, although I have seen bucks stand on their hind legs to reach higher branches. The buck will lick, nibble, chew and rub his face and antlers on the overhanging branch all the while depositing scent from his saliva, forehead glands, which are located near the antler bases, and the preorbital glands, which are located in the corner of each eye. I'm convinced, after having watched dozens of bucks make scrapes and many others visit scrapes, that the overhanging branch is the main communication center at any scrape. Many bucks that visit existing scrapes pay little attention to the scrape itself and may or may not urinate in it, but every buck I have ever seen visit a scrape has spent time working the overhanging branch. Sometimes a considerable amount of time.

Precisely what is communicated at the scrape is not known and probably never will be unless we can find a buck that will talk. But researchers suspect, and I agree, that scrapes are not, as some hunters believe, places where a doe can leave her scent so that a buck can then find her. Sure, the occasional doe will visit a scrape and sometimes even urinate in the scrape, but these visits appear to be purely by chance and not by design. Scrapes are a guy thing. They are places where bucks communicate with each other. My guess is that they are a whitetail version of a message board. And when a buck lays down a string of scrapes, he is letting every other buck around know that he considers himself to be top dog on that piece of turf.

If scrapes were only visited by the buck that originally made them, they would be

Hanging scent wicks around your stand does not take long and it might mean the difference between a shot and no shot when that big buck cruises through.

poor places to hunt. When you consider that at least 75 percent of all visits to scrapes are made at night, your odds of catching an individual buck visiting a scrape are very slim. But luckily for us hunters, it is common for more than one buck to visit a scrape or string of scrapes, which is generally called a "scrape line." I've seen a half-dozen different bucks visit the same scrapes during a single day on several different occasions, but even though I knew that multiple bucks will visit the same scrapes, I've got to admit that I was amazed when a surveillance camera situated near a large scrape photographed 21 different bucks visiting that scrape in a single night.

A mock scrape is one that you or I make in an attempt to encourage bucks to visit our handiwork. And it works. Not every time mind you. Nothing does when it comes to whitetail hunting. But the way I figure it, anything I can do to encourage a buck to make repeated visits to a specific location is going to boost the odds in my favor. Once a buck finds a mock scrape, that buck will make repeated visits to that scrape. Why, I'm not sure. If the buck is a mature buck, it is likely a matter of dominance. Sex appeal is almost certainly part of the equation. Curiosity too, I suspect. But the "why" is not so important to me. As long as I know that bucks will pay repeat visits to my mock scrapes, I'm in business.

You can go ahead and make your mock scrapes anytime you want prior to the season. I generally make mine in late spring or early summer. I know that serious scraping activity will not start until sometime in mid- to late October, but you don't want to wait until then to make mock scrapes. If you do, you have to compete with all of the real scrapes. You want your mock scrapes to be the first scrapes in the woods.

You can't make a mock scrape too early, but you can darn sure be too late, so make them well before the bucks start scraping and make them in places where the bucks can easily find them. Edges are always good. So are old logging roads. Ridges are one of my favorite locations. Bucks spend a lot of time on the high ground. If you are familiar with the area you hunt, you probably know where bucks have scraped in previous years. Put your mock scrapes there.

If there is not a suitable overhanging branch where you want to make a mock scrape, cut one from another tree and tie it to an existing branch or tree trunk so that it hangs about four to five feet above where you want to put the mock scrape.

A single mock scrape may get some attention, but a string of scrapes will get more. I like to put five to ten in a line or string. How far apart you space them depends upon the habitat and the terrain, but a scrape every 30 yards along an old logging road is not overdoing it.

When making a mock scrape, take precautions not to leave human scent in the area. Wear clean clothes and boots. Always wear gloves. Here is my recipe for effective mock scrapes.

Hang a scent wick on the overhanging branch and apply a liquid scent or a paste lure containing forehead gland to the wick. Rub a little scent on the branch itself.

Directly underneath the branch, use a garden trowel or stout stick to clear all grass and debris from a round or oval-shaped area about the size of a big beach ball. Bury an H.S. Buc-Rut Scent Wafer an inch or two under the surface. These scent-impregnated wafers slowly ooze scent and I have found that they will keep bucks coming back for a long time.

Pour about a cupful of Primetime Magic Scrape into the middle of the scrape. Magic Scrape is a waterproof, scent-impregnated soil that bucks find very appealing. In the center of that mound of Magic Scrape, make a depression and fill the depression with your favorite liquid scent. I've used buck urine, doe-in-estrous urine, buck urine with tarsal gland and others for this application and all seem to work just fine.

That's it. There is no need to go back to freshen up the scent. If there is a buck in the neighborhood, he will find the mock scrape and from then on, that buck and others will take care of adding their own scent to the overhanging branch and the scrape itself. You've made yourself a fine place to hang a stand.

AIRBORNE SCENTS

This is probably the least known and least practiced of all the different methods of using scents. I'll admit that it is a tactic that I do not use as much as the other methods of scent deployment we have discussed in this chapter. However, there are times when using airborne scents can make a huge difference. Airborne scents are simply scents that you spray into the air and let the air currents carry the scent to the deer. I use them in primarily two ways.

When hiking into my stand, I always have a spray bottle of scent handy. Let's say that on my route to my stand I must pass by a little off-shoot valley that is downwind

of me. I know that there are probably deer in that valley. So when I hike past it, I will saturate the air with mist from my spray bottle of scent. Perhaps it does nothing more than help to mask my own human odor. And if that is all that I accomplish, that is good enough for me. But if the time is right, the scent catches the attention of a nice buck, a buck that might just wander over in the direction from which the scent came. There, he will pick up the scent I have left on the ground with my drag rag and maybe, just maybe, he will follow that scent trail right to my stand.

The second way in which I employ an airborne scent is when a buck is getting downwind of my stand. This happens more often than I care to admit in a season and is especially commonplace when rattling. When I see that a buck is going to get downwind of me, I grab my spray bottle of scent and start pumping. Don't be cheap here. In fact, if you want to save some money you can water down your scents, but make sure that you saturate the air with scent. I generally use a good doe-in-estrous urine. Not only have I used this tactic successfully to prevent deer that were downwind from smelling me, but very often that deer has turned and marched right in.

Using deer scents anytime you are deer hunting makes sense to me, but when hunting during the rut, they are an invaluable tool.

Index

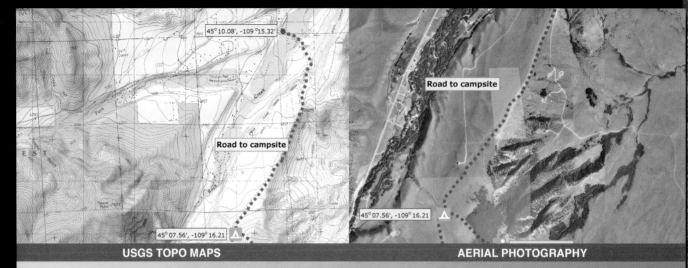